I0457685

JACK STORIES

Danny McKinney

Jack Stories

This book is written to provide information and motivation to readers. Its purpose is not to render any type of psychological, legal, or professional advice of any kind. The content is the sole opinion and expression of the author, and not necessarily that of the publisher.

Copyright © 2023 by Danny McKinney.

All rights reserved. No part of this book may be reproduced, transmitted, or distributed in any form by any means, including, but not limited to, recording, photocopying, or taking screenshots of parts of the book, without prior written permission from the author or the publisher. Brief quotations for noncommercial purposes, such as book reviews, permitted by Fair Use of the U.S. Copyright Law, are allowed without written permissions, as long as such quotations do not cause damage to the book's commercial value. For permissions, write to the publisher, whose address is stated below.

Printed in the United States of America.

ISBN   978-1-955363-96-9   (Paperback)
ISBN   978-1-955363-97-6   (Digital)

Lettra Press books may be ordered through booksellers or by contacting:

Lettra Press LLC
30 N Gould St. Suite 4753
Sheridan, WY 82801
1 307-200-3414 | info@lettrapress.com
www.lettrapress.com

TABLE OF CONTENTS

J ack's story is a blend of truth and fiction about a man who really lived, Jack McKinney. He lived from 1929-2015 in the Appalachian hills of east Tennessee. He and his family grew up poor among many other poor and struggling people during The Great Depression. He was my dad.

His was a simple life with many complications. His was a life with deep meaning for those with eyes to see and ears to hear. His lessons learned and relearned may be of some value to the reader today.

This book has grown as memories and ideas have flown in and out of my mind. A priceless gift today would be to sit with my dad for an hour or so and listen again to him tell of some of his various adventures. Further, I would seek his advice and also apologize to him for not understanding how brief our time together would be. This book is a gift to my dad. I believe that as all spirits return to God who gave them, that my Dad lives among The Great Cloud of Witnesses that together with us will celebrate a great home coming someday. We will stand around the throne of our Lord Jesus Christ, all eyes on him, but each of us grasping the hand of another who has perhaps gone before us or who has come after us. There will be no further longer or pining. All will be complete. So, not only will I see you then, Daddy, but I hope you like this now. I love you. Your son, Danny McKinney, March 3, 2021

PREFACE TO THE JACK STORY

After writing this little book about my dad, I found out that publishing companies are not interested so much in short story formats. Okay. That's okay. So, I am making a few changes to make this book more palatable for the world of readers. This collection of tales will now become a sweeping story of my dad's early life.

I loved my dad. It is true that sometimes I did not feel anything but frustration or anger toward him. I guess that is true of many people. But absence makes the heart grow fonder seems to be the truest of proverbs. God knows how sweet it would be to have a day out under the ceiling fan, creating a stir in the air that makes the afternoon heat tolerable. Just to listen to dad spin his yarns with his old friends. He talked freest with them. I would hope for an hour or so to ask him some questions about some aspects of his life that are unclear to me. Honestly, I would also love to get his advice on business dealings. He was very good at turning a buck on real estate.

When daddy died, that day as he was breathing out his last breaths, I had a chance to be alone with dad, among a house full of cousins and nieces and nephews, brothers and sister-in-law. I talked to daddy about things from the past, forgave him for offenses and asked him to forgive me of offenses that are sure to come between father and son over a lifetime. Then I talked to him about heaven. I reminded him that we are saved by the grace of God and not to go now in fear for His grace is sufficient to cover the likes of my dad and the likes of me. It was in Jesus

Christ that we placed our trust so many years ago when we confessed him before men and were baptized into his name for the forgiveness of sins. Sure, we messed up and thousand times over after that, but it was always Jesus that did the saving anyway. It is in him that we find rest from our efforts to save ourselves. And because of that, not any act of goodness or generosity on our parts, we are free to serve others and in so doing from time to time bring a smile to the God of heaven. The One who created us and the One in whom we were born in the image of.

I asked daddy to get word back to me. To let me know what it was like there in that great Cloud of Witnesses. I believe that when my daddy died that he was taken by the hand by his momma, my granny, Mayme McKinney. I believe that any fear he had as he breathed his last was allayed when he saw her smile and he heard her say is name for the first time since she died of a stroke, February 21,1989. I can just hear him call out "Mamma!" when he felt her hand in his and saw her smile. "Jack," she would have said. "Jack," and there was no reason to say anymore. Just that sealed the reunion as they knew one another in the land where we'll never grow old.

I wanted daddy to tell me if I had it at least partially right, and correct anything I have off base and further just explain to me what in the name of heaven is going on there after we die.

So far, no word from dad. You don't rush heaven. Heaven is on its own agenda. We find things out in God's good time. So, it is. But one day. One day I am convinced that God, who is a rewarder of those who diligently seek him, will give me that view of forever when I see his face at last. And then, when it seems gawking at him for eternity might be rude, I will see in my peripheral vision my family and friends who have gone on before. It will take a while to settle down all the shouting that is going to take place.

I hope you enjoy the way I have tied this collection of stories and lives together, now into one cohesive knot. Daddy was worth another shot.

So, let me begin. This is the story of a man's life. His name was Jack. Like most of our lives, it's mostly not real or in the words of the man himself, "It ought unreal." There comes a time in the lives of all men when, in the quieting of their minds, they realize that what has been happening to them in a series of troubles and joys and quiet times is their own life passing before them. Though we are active participants in it, there is a sense in which we are merely passive observers. Such was the case with Jack as he went from birth on a cold November morning to his dying breath in the hot summer days of August. Almost eighty-six years, most of which was lived in hopes of one day having a clear understanding of what this life is all about.

God was always there. Throughout his life, despite the fact that Jack made many attempts to follow his own path and leave God's ways behind, it was obvious, sometimes in snapshots of awe and wonder at what God could do, and sometimes in those late reflections that come on a person when they lie in bed at night and reflect on their lives, that God was there. God was before and behind. He was a constant fixture in Jack's life.

"Why me?" Jack would ask sometimes. "Lord, you know what a mess I have made of my life. I can't be any use to you. I can't read. I don't know the Bible like I should. I don't go to church like I should. I cuss like a sailor sometimes and I can't control my temper to save my soul. Why, Lord, are you still here? Why do I get this feeling that you love me despite all I've done? I don't deserve this."

Exactly. It is when one realizes that he has no capacity to save himself that he finds himself exactly where God needs for him to be. Jack, like me and you, needed a savior. He came to know that Jesus was the Savior of men. And that God's glory was the purpose of life. He came to understand that to help those in need was the hands-on approach to loving one's neighbor as one's self. Still, like us, he "walked by faith and not by sight," as the Good Book says. Who can do otherwise?

We who accompanied him on his journey grasp for scenes of his life in order to keep him alive in our memory. In those very efforts we find ourselves wandering if maybe we imagined the whole thing. It's like the fog of a dream awakened from; we know or at least believe it happened, but we can't quite seem to clear the fog of our minds to see it clearly. Any glimpse then is treasured, understood to be only a single frame in a lifelong movie. We gaze on it with satisfaction but not contentment. We long for more, even if it means our minds have to generate new or revised scenes in order to let the memory play on. That's what this story is all about. Grasping for the man Jack who was, is no more, yet lives on in our hearts.

Danny McKinney
January 25, 2019
March 3, 2021

CHAPTER ONE

A Happy Christmas

"What would it be like to see Santa Claus," Jack thought. Six-year-old Jack knew that children weren't supposed to see Santa. If they did, he supposed, something bad would happen. Maybe they would lose out on their special Christmas dinner or maybe they would end up with an empty stocking. Any way he looked at it, getting a glimpse of Old Santa would not end well. "How come seeing the nicest man on earth would end up being a bad thing?" Jack wondered.

The weeks prior to Christmas 1935 were full of excited talk among the kids at school. All of them were poor. All of them. Oh, some had more than others, but according to standards of an average American family today, they were destitute. They were smack dab in the middle of the Great Depression, after all. But the thing that was so weird for these Appalachian families, the ones who had money before the Depression and those who could read and had access to newspapers or had a radio to listen to, knew that these were hard times for people across the world. But for these people, used to growing their own food and making their own clothes, life went on just as it always had. Jack's teacher, Mrs. Seay, had decorated the classroom with cardboard stars the kids had cut out. She brought popcorn from home and had the students sew the corn into strings of garland that they strung around the classroom. Mrs. Seay even had Dillard Massengale, one of the older students at Englewood School, get a cedar tree from the edge of the field near the school, to use as a Christmas tree. This act was the one that really got the students excited. They sang Christmas songs during music class, fun ones like Jingle Bells, and beautiful ones, like Away in a Manger. Jack really wasn't much of a singer, but he found himself humming these little tunes later when he got home, either doing chores or when he and his brother, Dan, laid down to sleep at night. The boys would sing them together even. Amazing how the Spirit of Christmas brought out this harmony among the brothers and the other kids at school.

Mrs. Seay had the kids draw names so that they could all get a Christmas gift at school this year. For some of the kids, a gift from school would be the only gift they would get that Christmas. Oh, their mommas and daddies would have them gather black walnuts or hickory nuts to share together, maybe even making a black walnut cake from the meat of the nuts. The cake had a sharp taste, but the sugar and spice mixed in make the cake a particular favorite to many of the folks living out in these rural areas.

Sometimes the kids might find an apple and orange, maybe a piece or two of hard candy, or maybe even a penny or two down in the bottom of their stockings. The beautiful thing about these poor folks, is the appreciation they showed when such a stocking was received. They knew nothing of the entitlement that so many feel today. The preacher at church said one day, "It is not happy people that are thankful, but thankful people that are happy." That thought was a lot for a little boy to think about, but Jack rolled it around and around in his mind. His momma told the kids, "Children, we may not have much, but we can always have thankful hearts."

It's this kind of spirit that prevailed in Mrs. Seay's class at Englewood School. The kids were not to buy any gift. They had to make it. In this way no student was left out of being able to participate. Only boys drew boys' names, and girls drew girls' names. This kept kids from finding out whose name was drawn and then teasing the others about being boyfriend or girlfriend. It's mighty embarrassing to have your friends sing "Jack and Helen, sitting in a tree, K-I-S-S-I-N-G," for example.

When names were drawn, Jack drew Ross Martin's name. Ross lived in town and he was alright. He and Jack weren't best friends or anything, but at least he didn't get Johnny Linden's name. That Johnny had failed a couple of years and should have been in fourth grade. He had a habit of picking on the younger kids. It wasn't like he did outright mean things, it was just...oh, Jack couldn't hardly say. He just knew there was something about that boy that he didn't like.

Anyway, Jack had an idea. He was going to make a paddle ball game for Ross. Jack had a little rubber ball. It came from the inside of a baseball that Jack found out in the corner of the ball field. The ball had been there for a long time and with rain and weather, it was not any good anymore. But after Jack peeled off the hide and unstrung the thing, he found that it had a little rubber ball inside! The little ball was a great surprise. Jack played with it, bouncing it on the floor at home and against the wall before school started. The ball was a great toy, but Jack thought he could give it up in order to be able to have a gift for Ross. He would get a rubber band and cut it in two, then he would take a little board and attach the rubber band between the board and the ball. It was so wonderful how this idea came to Jack. It was like God just put this idea in his mind. Maybe God saw that Jack had a good heart about this Christmas gift and that was why he had such a good idea. Whatever the case, Jack had a plan and he was happy.

Often in life things don't always go as planned. But the crazy thing is that everything worked out just perfectly. I mean, when you consider that Jack was just six years old, it is pretty amazing that everything went right. Oh, maybe I forgot to mention that his teacher, Mrs. Seay, gave him the rubber band, and his dad, Lloyd, helped him attach the rubber band to the ball and the paddle. No matter how old we are, from six to ninety-six, we all need a little help sometimes. And sometimes it is just so much a part of our normal day to day lives that we miss the beauty of our relationships.

Jack got his momma to help him wrap up his present in newspaper and tie it together with string. He was beaming when he went to school that Friday before Christmas. The kids would have two weeks off from school and they were all excited about that. Add that to the excitement of the Christmas gift exchange and the cookies and apple cider that moms of some of the students brought--homemade cookies and apple cider! And mercy! All the kids were so happy. After the kids said the Pledge of Allegiance, Mrs. Seay had them all sit down so she could explain how the day was going to run. First, the kids were to make sure that when they opened their gifts, all the paper got picked up and placed in the trash can. Also, the students were to say only good things about gifts given or received. Mrs. Seay went by the slogan, "If you don't have anything good to say, don't say anything at all," and the Golden Rule, "Do unto to others as you would have them do unto you."

All the kids nodded their agreement and the passing out of gifts began. Mrs. Seay had all the presents place under the Christmas tree and she had chosen Margie Bowers to hand the gifts out to the kids as it came their turn. Margie was very shy and Mrs. Seay had chosen her to sort of pull her out of her shell. Margie's face was beet red, but everybody could tell that she was pleased as punch to have been chosen. She got down on her knees and looked up beaming at Mrs. Seay, ready to give out the gifts.

There was Allman, Bowers, Croft, Daugherty, and Eaton. It was a class of 26 children so it seemed to Jack that it took forever for the names to get around to Moses. There was Fain and Goins, Howell, Ingram, and Jack. Jack was a last name of Celia Jack, a cute little red headed girl in Jack's class. Every time Mrs. Seay would call "Jack" in the class, both Celia and Jack would look up.

Finally, they got around to the M's. Martin, there were two Martins in the class, and then Mrs. Seay called, "McKinney." Jack was confused. He was so excited about giving Ross Moses his gift that he had forgotten all about getting one himself. When Margie Bowers handed Jack his gift, wrapped in newspaper, just like the one he had for Ross, he could see it was from Johnny Linden. He looked up to see Johnny looking at him, leaning forward in anticipation of Jack opening the gift he brought for him. Jack cut the string his present was wrapped with and let the paper fall to the floor. It was a very small package, but when Jack saw what it was, he looked up at Johnny in amazement. It was a hand carved rabbit with long ears. Jack turned it around and around in his hands and everyone, including Mrs. Seay, was leaning in to have a closer look. Johnny explained. "My Uncle Bob helped me to whittle that out. I like working with wood. I wanted to carve out a rabbit with long ears. I figured it was just right for Jack to have a jack rabbit. There was a pause, and then everybody grinned and had a good laugh. Margie, still on her knees, looked up at Jack and said, "That's just right for Jack. He's so fast and full of energy. Just like a jack rabbit." Everybody was amazed to hear her speak. It was so out of character for her, but like everyone else that morning, she was caught up in the moment.

"Thank you, Johnny." Jack said. He had forgotten that he was even going to get a gift and then so surprised when the one kid in the class that he really didn't like gave him a gift that was just perfect for him, he was taken aback.

Jack was still looking at Johnny when Mrs. Seay said, "Moses," and Margie handed Ross Moses his gift. Jack looked in at Ross as he opened his gift, anxious to see if he would like it. When the paper came off and Ross realized he had a paddle board, he began playing with it immediately. He grinned and looked up at Jack. "Gee, thanks, Jack. This is fun!" And he continued to bounce the ball off the paddle while other kids begged Ross for a turn.

After all the gifts were handed out, the mothers handed out cookies and hot apple cider to the kids and they all fell into a relaxed and happy mood. The kids got to go home at lunch on this last day of school before Christmas break so even Mrs. Seay was able to relax and think about those two wonderful weeks that lay before her. She loved here students, but she was due a break and well deserving of it. She had once again made a day full of special memories for the children. It was a gift that she kept giving to students year after year for over forty years. She made the town of Englewood a little richer. She gave children like Jack and Johnny and Margie the chance to be more than even they knew they were. The memories she gave these little ones were held close in their hearts as long as they lived. In his later years, Jack would remember this day, and think about how badly he had wanted to see Santa Claus but was afraid to for fear of what might happen. It dawned on him that, when he looked in the face of Mrs. Seay, he was looking into the face of Santa. Santa, it turns out, is just too big to be captured in a red suit with a fur collar. Santa is a spirit that lives in the hearts of those who look outside themselves, using their lives to bless others. That's what Mrs. Seay embodied and that is the spirit that the children shared on that Christmas so long ago, 1935.

When the kids went home that day, they rushed out of school and off toward their homes, the tunes of "Jingle Bells" and "Away in a Manger" carrying them all the way home.

CHAPTER TWO

Shiny New Nickel

Some time passed from that scene at school in Mrs. Seay's classroom. The sweet moment remained a memory for Jack for the rest of his life. In fact, out of season or not, Jack was thinking about that very thing while he was walking home from town one day all by himself. The world Jack grew up in was much safer in many ways than it is today. A kid waking the dirt road was a common sight. His mother had sent the kids to take a paper bag (they called it a "poke" because you had to poke your hand down in it to open it up) full of tomatoes to their Aunt Thelma. Ant Thelma lived in town over by the railroad tracks in a little white wood-sided house. After the tomato delivery, Jack's brother, Dan, and four sisters, Jean, Denny, Margaret, and Tommy had all raced home to see a new puppy they'd found outside their door that morning. Living in the country it was not the strangest thing to find a pup outside your door-in fact, it happened all the time. People who lived in town would drop unwanted pups or even full-grown dogs out in the country and just drive away. There were no animal shelters in those days; at least not in McMinn county.

So, his brother and sisters ran on ahead but Jack held back. He was thinking about a Satchel Paige baseball card his buddy, Winston, had. He showed it to Jack that morning and offered to sell it to him for a nickel if he wanted it. Wanted it? Satchel Paige played in the Negro Leagues of professional baseball and boy, was he good. He played for the Chattanooga Black Barons, which was a big town down south of where Jack and his family lived. Nobody knew exactly how old he was, not even Satchel himself. Lots of folks didn't keep up with dates and documents as much back in those days. Growing up poor made other things more important. Like keeping wood cut to heat the house and crops gathered to feed the family. That was why Jack was thinking about Christmas. If it was Christmas, maybe somehow or other, he could wake up and find that Satchel Paige card in his stocking. He knew it would never happen, but how wonderful a thing the imagination was. One could envision just about anything they wanted, see life anyway they could imagine, and it their minds, at least, for a time, it would be just like it was real. Jack was looking at that card and just smiling ear to ear. Santa had brought him the very thing he wanted most. What a lucky boy he was! The depression might have taken away the opportunity to earn money for a lot of people, but it could not take away the gift of imagination.

Anyway, Jack felt he could relate to Satchel. Here was someone that was poor and had trouble in school, like him. Jack couldn't read well (or at all, really). He wondered what trouble Satchel might have had trying to learn. Anyway, he was someone who had life against him, but would one day become one of the best-known baseball players of all time. Now Jack didn't play baseball. Unfortunately, he never got an opportunity to play sports. He always had school and then work when he came home. Besides for regular chore of splitting wood for his mother's cook stove, he and his brother, Dan, had in mind to cut some wood of their own and have it available to sell to town folks during the winter months. They were already asking around to see who might be interested in buying firewood from them. They had a couple of folks in town say they might be interested, if the wood was cured/dry and was cut small enough to fit in their cook stoves. Hopefully, then, the work Jack and Dan were doing could possibly pay off someday and they were anxious for that to happen. In the meantime, on Saturdays when they could pick up a game, they'd listen to the radio station that broadcasted the

Chattanooga Black Barons and always cheered for Satchel. They knew the names of several of the other players, and many of them were good too, but it was Satchel they cheered for. Jack planned to make it big one day, Just like Satchel. No matter what anyone said. He didn't voice out his dreams. No, he held them tight. Some might see such things as bragging or just plain foolishness, so it was better to just keep one's personal aspirations to one's self.

Just then, something bit Jack on the leg. A horse fly had somehow gotten up in the pants leg of his overalls and bit the tar out of him! Jack swatted his leg several times and then shook the dead horsefly out of his pants' leg. It's pretty amazing how something as simple as a horsefly can bring you back to earth in a flash! Well, as Jack bent down to scratch the place on his leg, he saw something shiny on the ground. Right there on that dusty road lay a shiny new nickel! It was like the heavens opened up and smiled on him! He reached down and picked up a 1936 Buffalo nickel. Someone must have lost it walking along the way to town. The way Jack saw it, it was his nickel now. You know, finders, keepers, losers, weepers. Besides, there was no way to know who that nickel belonged to. All Jack knew, was that it was his nickel now. Now he could buy that card from Winston! Jack looked forward and back. If he hurried, maybe he could catch up with Winston and buy that Satchel Paige baseball card right now before someone else bought it. If he went back for the baseball card, he might get in trouble for not coming straight home from delivering the tomatoes to Aunt Thelma, like he was supposed to. Why did life have to be so complicated? If he only knew how complicated it was going to get that day, he'd have kept that thought for later.

Finally, Jack decided to risk it. He had to have that card and he'd risk a whipping or extra chore in order to get it. Now remember, this was long before cell phones were ever even thought of. In fact, Jack's family, like most others in those days, didn't even own a phone! If someone had to make a call, they had to come into town and borrow the phone at the general merchandise store.

So, Jack ran. He was pretty fast for his age. He had won many a race against his classmates during recess. He ran like the Dickens, as they say, and was breathing hard when he spotted Winston across Main Street over at the train depot. He was showing his cards off to another boy they went to school with, Charlie Wilson. Charlie always had money and was showing off with his candy cigarettes and jaw breakers. His daddy owned a drug store in town and always gave Charlie a fifty-cent piece every week for spending money. Fifty cents! It wasn't fair that some were so rich and others seemed to have nothing, but that was the way it was.

Just then, Mrs. Daugherty came out of the General Merchandise. Jack noticed the usually cheerful lady and said Hello to her. She didn't even seem to notice he was there. In a little town like Englewood everyone knew everyone else or at least their people. Jack had known Mrs. Daugherty all his life. He knew her kids, they were some younger than him, and he knew right where they lived. It was just a half mile or so from their place. "Everything all right, Mrs. Daugherty?" he asked.

"Huh?" she said. She seemed startled not realizing anyone was there. "Oh, Jack. How are you? I didn't even see you there."

"I'm fine, Mrs. Daugherty." Jack replied. "Is everything, all right? Is there anything I can help you with?"

"No, no," Mrs. Daugherty said. I just walked into town to get some sugar for my apple spice cake and when I got here, I came up a little short of the money I needed, that's all. I counted it out before I left the house but I must have dropped it somewhere along the road. I guess we'll just have to do without this time."

Jack swallowed. "How much did you lose, Mrs. Daugherty?" He asked.

"Oh, it was just a nickel but I counted out to the penny how much I needed with none to spare. It's okay, Jack. Mr. Culberson is about to close up in a few minutes anyway. I just wanted to bake that cake for Bonnie's birthday. You know she's been awful sick lately," she said.

Jack looked across the street at Winston who was still talking to that Wilson boy. Man! Why did life have to be so complicated? Then he looked back at Mrs. Daugherty. "Mrs. Daugherty, it's okay. You can still buy the sugar you need. Look what I've got!" Jack opened his hand and showed Mrs. Daugherty the nickel.

"Well, Jack, I can't take your nickel. You're a sweet boy and all, but that's your nickel. We'll be alright," she said.

Jack looked once more across the street as it appeared that Charlie was handing money to Winston and Winston was handing Charlie baseball cards in return. Jack sighed but he knew this was the right thing to do. "Mrs. Daugherty, I was just on my way home when I found this nickel on the road that leads to your house and mine. It's got to be your nickel. Here, take it and go buy your sugar."

Mrs. Daugherty looked at Jack in amazement. "Well, I declare, Jack. You have to be the kindest boy ever! God bless you. You wait till I see your momma. I've always liked your momma, but I had no idea what good kids she had. Mercy sakes, boy. Let me give you a hug."

Jack let Mrs. Daugherty hug him right there for all to see. Normally he'd have been embarrassed to let folks see him like that, but today, well, today, he felt so good about what he'd just done, especially after what Mrs. Daugherty said about his mother. Jack felt so good he'd have hugged himself if Mrs. Daugherty hadn't done it for him.

So, this is what being good felt like? Maybe heaven really was smiling down on him. And as for Satchel Paige baseball card, well, surely there would be another time for that.

CHAPTER THREE

Cowboy's Cow Ride

Most people don't ride cows. Jack knew that. Well, he knew that there were cowboys out west that liked to try their hand at roping calves and tying their back hooves off in competitions for some reason—he hadn't thought much about it before but it must have been because they were bored. Jack could understand doing crazy things when he was bored. It had been a while since he'd done the right thing by Mrs. Daugherty. He was still glad he did it but sometimes he thought about that Satchel Paige card. He could sure enough have whiled away the hours studying it and dreaming what it might be like to be a pitcher in the Big Leagues.

Jack was walking along the barbed wire fence that ran beside the stream that came out of the spring that flowed from under a big rock over on the Casteel's place. He was looking for water snakes. Sometimes they called them water moccasins but they weren't really. They weren't the poisonous kind. Or at least he didn't think so. At least they didn't have that triangular shaped head he had heard poisonous snakes had. Anyway, Jack was hoping to find some of these snakes so he could take a rock or piece of glass and throw it at them and knock them off the barbed wire fence or, if he was lucky, even kill them. It wasn't baseball, but if he could knock a snake off a barbed wire with a piece of glass, well, that was something.

Now you might ask why Jack would want to do that and the answer is simple. He was bored. And when you're bored you have to use your imagination to get you out of your predicament. He usually had to be hoeing corn or mounding dirt up on the potato hills or putting Sevin dust on tomato plants to keep the bugs off but today no one was there to see to it that he got it done. His momma and daddy had gone over to Riceville to see his daddy's parents. His daddy's momma was sick so they'd gone to help. They left Jack's brother, Dan, in charge of the kids, but Dan didn't have the heart to make the other kids mind, and besides, if they hurried, the six of them could knock the work out that needed done in a jiffy. So, they were all just hanging around. The girls were playing house out in the woods. They didn't have much more than their imagination, but that was enough to lay pine branches out to create rooms and pine needles to make beds. Then they'd assign one to be momma, that was always Jean, and Tommy had to play the part of baby sister. Sometimes Denny and Margaret would be one of the boys or maybe a neighbor that came by or one of the grandparents. They would play house for hours. Nobody came by to tell them they didn't have anything and should be sad. Their make-believe world was more fun than anything bought in a store and a lot more readily available.

Dan was trying to knock a squirrel down out of a tree (everyone wanted to be a ball player when spring came) alongside the pasture when Jack came by. "What you doing?" Jack asked.

"Bowser (that the name of their dog) here has treed a squirrel in this poplar tree and I'm trying to knock him out with some rocks. Maybe we could cook him up for supper. Some squirrel stew sounds pretty good to me about now," Dan replied.

"Yeah," Jack said, and he joined his brother, Dan, in trying to knock the squirrel out of the tree with rocks. They pelted the tree with rocks. They barely missed knocking each other in the head a few times with rocks. They scared the dog with rocks so bad that he ran off a piece more than once only to ease back to the squirrel scene, barking his head off and jumping up on the tree. If this tree had been like most around there, all clumped together in a forest of trees, that squirrel would have high-tailed it, jumping one tree to the next until those boys were only in its hickory nut sized mind's memory. But of course, he'd been jumped so quickly by Bowser that he'd hit the nearest tree to him, this lonely poplar out in the bottom pasture. Lucky for the squirrel Jack and Dan were no baseball players after all, at least not today. They finally gave up.

Jack said "That old squirrel isn't going anywhere. Bowser here will keep him holed up in that tree till Michael's trumpet blows. Let leave him be and come back and check on him later. I was looking for snakes on the fence line to knock off. You want to see what we can find?"

"Sure," Dan responded. "I nailed one yesterday just above the stream there as it comes under the bridge. I got him with a piece of old pop bottle. I cut him right in two. He fell off in the water and I run down to get him but he slithered away. How can those things be nearly cut clean in two and still be alive enough to swim off like that? It doesn't make no sense to me."

"Me neither," Jack said. "Some old crow flew down and got him, most likely, and ate him for supper. He appreciates your help."

"Yeah. Maybe so," Dan said.

Just then Rosie came sauntering across the pasture. Rosie was a Black Angus cow that their uncle had put in the pasture a little while back. Uncle Ray lived in a little shack of a house on the other end of the pasture. He said he traded an old hunting knife and five dollars for Rosie. She wasn't much, it didn't appear. Just an old black cow, but to two boys with nothing to do she presented a challenge.

"I bet you won't ride her," Dan said, their snake hunt immediately forgotten.

"I bet you won't ride her. You're two years older than me and supposed to be nearly grown up. You ride her," Jack challenged back.

"Nope, no fair. I said it first. If you don't ride her, I'm going to tell everybody you're afraid of an old cow. You're the fighter in the family. Besides, you could say you was a real cow wrangler if you got up on that cow and just rode her one minute," Dan said.

"Okay," Jack said. "I'll tell you what. I'll ride her and then you ride her and we'll see who can stay on her longest."

"Deal!" Dan said back. "I'll hold her while you get on." The boys pulled up some green grass from outside the fence and offered it to Rosie. She looked at the boys, considered their offer, concluded that there wasn't much else going on, and sauntered over to accept their gift. While Jack let Rosie eat the grass from his hand, Dan began petting her and then slid his hands over her head and under her jaw. Jack grabbed the loose skin behind her ears and pulled himself up in one mighty lunge. There was a surprised look in Rosie's eyes and then the more than a thousand-pound Black Angus had her say. She bellowed and began to rush madly around the pasture. It was Jack's turn to have crazy eyes. His brother Dan was laughing his head off! Jack was holding on for dear life and Rosie was intent on getting that pest off her back.

Dan yelled out, "You're a real cowboy now, Jack!" and began busting up laughing again.

Jack didn't say anything intelligible. His sounds of "Ohhh!" and "aughh!" Were drowned out by Rosie's rage and Dan's delight. Finally, Rosie raced toward the poplar tree Bowser had treed the squirrel in. Jack tried to bale off. He just knew she was so mad she might just run smack into that tree, killing herself and him. Just as he was making his move to throw himself off Rosie sort of bucked and shifted him back to her left side and right into the poplar tree! Rosie ran triumphantly and angrily on to the other end of the pasture. Dan's laughter turned to shock when he heard the crunch of Jack's ribs against the poplar tree. He ran to Jack who just lay there at the base of the tree moaning, his hands wrapped around himself and blood trickling from his mouth. His eyes were squinted shut in pain. Jack had bitten his tongue near clean off with the impact and had broken and cracked several ribs in the process. He moaned as Dan knelt down beside him.

"Oh no, Jack! Are you okay?" Isn't it crazy how we ask such ridiculous questions at times like this? His brother is laying at the base of a tree that he just hit full blast off the back of an angry Black Angus cow. He's lying there on the ground wrapping himself up, moaning, with blood coming from his mouth and we say silly stuff like: "Are you okay?"

Anyway, Jack opened his eyes, looked at his brother Dan, gave a half grin in between the jolts of pain that racked his body and said, "How long did I ride her?"

Dan sat back bewildered. "How long did you ride her? I don't know. Are you crazy? You're lying here nearly killed and you want to know how long you stayed on? Are you even going to be alright? Momma's going to kill us."

Jack thought a minute. He looked up at Dan and whispered out through clinched teeth: "I'll be…okay. We won't tell Momma. But Dan, I don't think you ought to ride Rosie. She doesn't much like it and one cowboy in the family is enough." Bowser barked his agreement.

CHAPTER FOUR

Big Day on the Town

Two weeks passed before the boys even thought of doing something questionable. Broken ribs are no joke, but Jack did his best to act as if there was no problem at all.

His momma noticed he was getting around a bit stiffly (mothers miss nothing after all). "Jack, son, have you hurt yourself some kind of way?" she asked one morning after the family had sat down to a breakfast of biscuits and gravy, sausage and eggs. The rest of the family had already gone on to their business, leaving Jack and his mother a rare moment together, just the two of them.

"I'm okay, Momma. Just a little stiff this morning. Maybe I slept a little crooked or something last night."

Mayme studied her boy a little further. "Well," she said, "Just make sure you stretch those muscles out good before you get to work this morning."

"Yes ma'am. I will" He started to take just a little stretch right there in front of her and then winced in pain. "Yes ma'am. I sure do need to stretch." He smiled a little smile back at her. Both of them knew that she didn't buy the "I slept a little crooked" line but Mayme let it go. She knew that boys would be boys and were bound to get banged up from time to time.

"Just see to it that you're not getting into fights that you have no business in."

"No ma'am. I won't. I'll behave, Momma," Jack said as he hurried on out the door.

The next morning all the kids were sitting at the breakfast table eating pancakes with some of their Momma's homemade syrup. There wasn't any store-bought syrup to be had in those days, especially where Jack and his family lived. "They were too poor to pay attention," as some people say. Most folks up in the knobs where they lived didn't have much so they didn't go on about not having things. Momma would say "We don't cry and go on when we don't have things. We make do with what we've got." And with that mentality God always seemed to put the things they needed in their hands just when they needed them most.

And so, it was with Momma's syrup. And boy, it was good. She'd heat it up on the cook stove and it would pour down on those pancakes like it was off to the races. The kids would sop it up with every bite and when they were finished eating-Mercy! They didn't feel like poor folks but rich as kings and queens living in a house surround and infiltrated with Momma's love. Jack looked up at Momma and thanked her for the fine breakfast. All the kids chimed in their agreement.

Dan said, "Momma, what you want us to do today? Hoe those potatoes in that upper field or thin out that sweet corn up on the hill? I was also noticing that the tobacco up by the barn will need hoed and maybe have some fertilizer worked in around it here pretty quick."

"That's good thinking, son, all of it," Momma said. "And we'll get to all that in due time. But today I want you kids to weed my strawberry patch. Be careful not to pull up the plants. Don't be using no hoes. All this works got to be done by hand. If youn's get them weeds out good we are about to have us a wonderful batch of strawberries this year. We'll have strawberry jam and pie; we'll have strawberry dumplings and even some sugar sweet strawberries to put on your pancakes! It's fix'n to be good, Lord-willing. You take care of what God gives you and He'll take care of you." Momma always was good to give God credit for things. She taught them how all things worked together for good for them that loved the Lord. This was long before anyone in those parts was talking about ecosystems and such. The kids just knew that the land provided for their needs when they took care of the land. Momma went on: "When youn's finish, if you do a good job, how'd you like to go into town?" There was such a clamor at the table. Chairs were scuffing and Jean liked to fell clean back in hers if Margaret hadn't of caught her.

"We'll get it done, Momma," Jack said. "We'll do such a good job you won't ever know that there were any weeds in that patch." All the kids' bright faces showed their agreement.

"Jack, have you got those kinks worked out enough to be able to pull weeds?"

"yes, Momma." Jack said. "I'll be fine. I'll sit down on the ground if I have to, but I will do my share."

"I know you will, son. All right, then. Off with the lot of you. I'll be up there directly to check on your work. I'll keep little Tommy here with me. She can help me with the work here at the house, can't you Tommy?" Tommy was barely three years old and there were lots of things she wasn't quite ready to help out with yet, but you could hardly tell her that.

"Momma," she said in her tiny voice, "I want to go with them."

"Not today, sweetheart. You're going to stay here and help Momma. Now go out there on the porch and get Momma a basket of them cucumbers. Go on now. We have to get this work done before we go into town." Tommy had a little frown on her face. She still wanted to go with the big kids, but she'd mind Momma.

"Okay, Momma. I'll hurry," she said. "Meantime, I'll be getting some of these cucumbers canned. You boys can carry them up to the shed after a while for safe keeping. Hurry now. I'll be up there in a little bit."

The kids were already out the door and advancing quickly on the strawberry patch. You never seen such an eager bunch. They couldn't wait to go into town. Who knows who they might see and Momma might even come up with a few pennies so they could buy some candy? Mostly they'd get some rock candy and maybe an orange or apple for Christmas. Sometimes maybe even a penny would be in their stocking, but every now and then, they'd have such occasions as this. Just out of the blue they'd get to go into town. Jack figured they'd been maybe twice before that he remembered.

"Hey Dan. How many times you been into town that you can remember?" Jack asked his older brother.

"We went last spring, you remember? Momma had to go into town to get some jar lids for canning." Momma used these canning jars over and over but sometimes the lids would just give out and had to be replaced. If you didn't get a good seal, all that work would be for nothing.

"Yeah, I remember that," Jack said. "And I remember one time, maybe three or four years ago we had to go find Dr. Foree. Remember that? Denny's head was just a splitting and Momma had done all she knew to do to help her. You remember that, Denny?"

Denny thought a minute. She wasn't but seven years old now. "I remember getting some bad headaches, that's for sure. I still have 'em," She said back.

"We'll this time," Jack responded, "You was crying and pitiful. Couldn't nobody get no sleep and I felt so sorry for you I just begged Momma to get Doc Foree. She said we couldn't afford it, but, you know, Doc Foree is so good. He'll come to the house if you could get hold of him and he'll take a dozen eggs or sack of corn in trade for his services if you can't pay." All the kids knew about Doctor Foree. When he was mentioned there was a sense of reverence for the man. All knew that without the Doc they'd be in a whole heap of trouble.

Dan went on. "Seems like we went into town a time or two before for some reason but I was too young to know why."

As they talked, the kid's little hands were busy working the weeds away from the strawberry plants without uprooting them. Every now and then a plant would get pulled up with the weeds around it but then they'd tuck it gently back into the ground. These kids knew that the land provided for them and so they made sure to pay attention to what they were doing. It made the difference between eating good and doing without.

Momma came down to the patch just as they were finishing their work. "Let's take a look at what you young'un have got done here," She said. "Looks pretty good. Jack reach there and get that weed yonder. Good. What else? See them weed in there, Jean? There you go. Make sure to get all them out." She went on around the garden patch with a careful eye. "Nice job. Looks to me like you kids want to go into town."

"Yes, ma'am!" they all cried, bouncing up and down like a store full of Jack-in-the Boxes.

"We'll, Jack, you and Dan get on down to the barn and hook up the wagon. The rest of you kids get up to the pump there and wash your hands and faces good. Don't forget to wash them nasty feet." Momma always wanted them to make sure they looked clean at least when they went anywhere. "People can't help what they've got to wear," she'd say, "but you don't have to go looking like you don't know how to keep yourself clean. That's just common decency."

In a little while the boys had their horse, Jenny, hitched to the wagon and brought it around by the house for everyone to load up. They helped Momma up in the bench seat and loaded the rest of the kids up in the back. Margaret was holding Tommy on her lap to make sure she didn't spill out on the bumpy road. Dan took his place driving the brood into town. It was a good way into town and would take them an hour in and an hour back, not to mention taking care of their business while they were there. Overall, a trip into town took a pretty good bite out of the day. It was mid-morning when they started out.

"Momma, reckon I can drive Jenny when we're coming home? These girls will drive me crazy back here," Jack said. They all gave him a look.

"Us drive him crazy?" Jean said.

"Yeah!" Margaret responded. "If anybody is going to go crazy, it's us!"

"We'll see," Momma said. "We'll see." And then she set off singing "When the Roll is called up Yonder" and all the kids joined in. They sang and laughed all the way to town. It seemed like they hardly got started before they were there.

First thing you know the kids were saying, "There's Mrs. Johnson," and "Hey, Winston! What you doing?" The excitement was brewing when they finally dismounted. What a beautiful day it was and Momma had brought them to town. They went first to Joe Baskett's Mercantile. Momma bought her canning lids from him. They went on down the street to Daddy Bryant's General Store. He kept a supply of hard candy that made the kids' mouths' water. Mercy! When they went in there they didn't care if they ever left! Bright colored candies in clear glass jars and all selling for pieces on the penny!

Jean went right up to the counter where Daddy Bryant's wife had just been talking with a customer. "And what can I get for you, young lady?" She asked.

"I want a red penny's worth of candy!" She declared.

Mrs. Bryant held back a chuckle. "Oh, you do, do you? Well, that sure is a nice-looking penny. Where'd you come up with such a nice-looking piece?" She asked, smiling.

"My Momma gave it to me. She gave each one of us kids a penny for helping weed out the strawberry patch."

"I'll say. You sure do have a good momma, don't you?" Mrs. Bryant answered back.

"Yes, ma'am. Nobody ever had a better momma than ours," Jean said with conviction.

Momma was perusing some things on the shelf but she heard every word and it was one of those moments that made all the trouble of raising six kids worth it. At that moment, she wouldn't have traded places with any woman in the world.

"All right then," said Mrs. Bryant. She took a small paper bag and went over to her candy jars. While the little dark haired Jean watched in amazement, Mrs. Bryant put candy in the bag from three different jars and then fold up the top and handed it down to Jean.

"Thank you, Mrs. Bryant," was all Jean could manage to say. She knew Mrs. Bryant had given her an awful lot of candy for a red penny. None of this had escaped Momma's notice either.

"Mrs. Bryant," Momma started, but Mrs. Bryant cut her off. "I know, ma'am. I know. But a woman who has kids as mindful as yours are and what loves their momma the way they do deserve a little extra reward."

With a tear in her eye Momma nodded her consent. "Thank you, Mrs. Bryant. There wouldn't be no Englewood if it weren't for such as you and your husband. And as far as my kids are concerned, I am a blessed woman."

There was more candy bought by the other kids and Momma got some sugar while they were there, but in a little while it was time to get back on the wagon and head home. Momma let Jack do the driving and everyone settled in to singing "She'll be coming around the Mountain When She Comes."

Jack let his mind run free. Here he was driving a wagon load of kids home with a woman beside him that barely had the means to get by but somehow, she not only did so but had a way of making all them enjoy it as the days went by. He didn't know what would become of him someday. What kind of work he'd be doing or where he'd be living or even who he'd marry. All that could be dealt with another day or in the quiet moments before he went to sleep at night. But for right now, he just wanted to bask in the beauty and simplicity of being one with his family. Momma, brother, sisters and all.

CHAPTER FIVE

Bowser, a Cast Away Dog finds a Home

Growing up the McKinney family had lots of dogs. Out in the country so many people dropped their dogs off and then left them to fend for themselves. Many of those dogs ended up in the homes of the country folks. Out in the country people generally didn't keep their dogs put up. They ran free and did as they wanted. You might think these dogs, once claimed, would just run away, but for the most part, they didn't. They knew two things: who loved them and where their food came from. So, even if they took off after rabbits or running with other dogs during the day, they always came home at night. And mostly they hung close to the house so they could be with their people. And with Jack and other country boys like him, adventures were never far away.

Jack's favorite dog, for all his life, was Bowser. Bowser was just one of those strays that someone from town dropped off, but from the day he came to their home, Bowser knew Jack and his brother and sisters were his and he was theirs. This is the story of how Bowser came to live with Jack and his family.

One morning Jack was up at dawn checking for eggs in the hen house when he looked up and saw this mangy dog, maybe a year or so old looking up at him, hoping for a hand out. It was plain that if breakfast didn't come from Jack's hand this dog would be giving these hens a run for their lives the minute he was out of sight. "What you say there, dog?" Jack asked. "You sure are a rough looking character. It's a wonder someone hadn't taken a bullet to you. Mercy, at the mange. What's your name anyway?"

The dog looked at Jack and barked. "Bow, bow, bow wow!"

"You don't say?" Said Jack. "Bow, bow, bow wow is quiet a name. Would you mind if I shortened it and just called you Bowser?"

The dog looked again at Jack and turned his head side to side, as if he were thinking about it. Then again, he barked out, "Bow wow!"

"Alright then," Jack said. "We'll have to work on you saying it right, but that was a good start. In the meantime, I've got to get these eggs up to the house and get back out here and do the milking, and then have some breakfast, but in a little while, we got to get you doctored up. You look pitiful. Mercy, at the mange. Bless your heart, but don't you worry, I've got just the concoction needed to get you all fixed up."

Jack hurried on backup to the house where Momma had bacon and eggs, cornbread and gravy. There was some of Momma's muscadine jelly on the table, along with some butter they had churned up just the day before. It was going to be a good day, for sure and for certain. Jack kind of kept an eye out, and an ear pealed. He wanted to be sure that this new dog didn't have his breakfast at the expense of their few chickens.

After the chores were finished and breakfast eaten, Jack slipped down to the barn with a pail of old burnt oil that old man Masey had drained out of his John Deere tractor. Jack smiled when he thought of them great ole big steel tires that thing had and how it left a smoke trail like a locomotive. "Must be nice to have that kind of money and not have to hitch up a horse or mule to pull a turning plow with," he thought. But then when he thought of their horse, Jenny, he figured if it come down to it, he'd keep her and say no to that big contraption. Working with Jenny might be more of a hassle, be he loved her. They all did. It seemed to Jack that she loved them back, the way she'd lay her head over on him when he went out to brush her or feed her at night. No, he'd never trade Jenny for machine or money. Some things just couldn't be bought.

Snapping out of his trance, Jack saw Bowser peering out from behind the barn. He was still trying to find himself something to eat. Jack had sneaked him out a piece of cornbread and reached it out to him. He nearly took his hand off! "Easy, boy," he said. I should have known better than that. I guess you're starved to death. But look here. I'll get you some more eats, but right now we got to take care of that ole mange. Now hold still a minute." And with that, Jack began to take an old rag and rub the burnt oil gently onto Bowser's mange. It almost covered his whole body. "Bless your heart," Jack said over and over. "My goodness, little boy. Don't you worry. I know this is quite a mess but it will heal you right up. I don't know what it is about it, but this stuff somehow suffocates that mange and then your hair will grow back good as new. I've seen it work lots of times."

Just then, Jean came around the house, followed by Denny and Margaret. Margaret had little Tommy on her hip. "A dog! Where'd you get this old dog? It's got the mange something awful!" Jean said.

"I know," Jack said. "But this stuff will heal him right up and I bet he'll be a pretty dog, won't you, Bowser?"

"Bowser? What kind of silly name is that? Let's call her Molly, after Molly with Fiber McGee!" Jean shouted.

Margaret and Denny both agreed by nodding their heads and saying "Yeah! Molly would be a great name."

Tommy just laughed and said "A puppy!"

"No, I done named him Bowser, and that's it," Jack said, defiantly. "Besides, this dog is a 'he'."

"What's all this commotion about?" Momma said, rounding the corner of the barn. "You children are needed out in the field picking beans and cutting off okry.

"We will, Momma," Jack said. "But looky here. Somebody dropped this dog off on our place and he had the mange and I was doctoring him up."

Momma came closer and walked around the dog. "Mercy, he sure has a bad case of the mange, but Jack, you are doing just the right thing to help him. He ought to heal up all right. Reckon you could train him to be useful around here? We can't be having a dog that don't pull his weight."

Jack and Dan chimed in together. "Momma, we'll teach him good, you'll see." The boys smiled a t one another in agreement.

"Just look at his eyes, Momma. He's a smart one. Thank you, Momma, and we'll take real good care of him. Won't we, Dan?"

"You bet we will. He's going to be the best dog ever," Dan said.

"Hey, what about us? He's going to be our dog, too, ain't he Momma?" The girls shouted out.

"Well, of course he will be the dog for the whole family if he can mind his manners. What do you reckon we ought to name him?" Momma asked.

Jean jumped in. "Momma we want to name her Molly after Fiber McGee and Molly. Wouldn't that be great? But Jack, He gave her this ole dumb name, Bowser."

"And I pointed out that this dog is not a she," Jack said.

"Bowser, is it? I had a dog named Bowser when I was a little girl. He was the best dog we ever had. He'd bring in the goats and run off all the other strays dropped off at out step. We never lost a chicken or worried about trash being drug out in the yard. I think Bowser is a great name." And with that, Bowser it was. The girls wouldn't defy Momma on her choice. It wasn't so much they were afraid of their Momma; they were in awe of her. There's more to be said of her than can be told here, but be sure that Momma had those kids wrapped around her little finger and none of them wanted to get loose.

The kids' dad, Lloyd, had been up at the smoke house getting down a ham they were planning to cook for supper. Mayme cut a slab off it and handed it to Dan.

"Son, run this back up to the smoke house and hang it back up for next time. Tonight, I am going to make some pinto beans and cornbread, along with this smoked ham and a mess of greens. I reckon I'll also fry up some okry and boil a pan of green beans to finish off the meal." The whole family was looking at her with light in their eyes. Law, they were going to eat good tonight!

Once Dan had the ham put back up and came out of the smoke house, he saw Momma and Daddy and Jack and the girls all congregated around something near the barn.

"What's a going on down here?" He asked.

"Well, what can we say? We have a new dog for the family and Momma said we could keep it and we're going to call him Bowser," Jean said, as if she had been appointed family reporter.

"Boy, it sure does have a bad case of the mange, but that old burnt oil will take care of that. Maybe we can make a hunting dog out of him, reckon, Jack?"

"Sure," Jack said. "I bet he can hunt and watch the place and everything!" All the kids were beaming and Momma and Daddy, too. It is an amazing thing how a little love can take such humble beginnings and craft from them a beautiful thing. Amidst all this, Bowser looked up from his burnt oil bath and barked. He may have had a bad start, but he felt the family's love and returned it. He washed Jack's face to show his appreciation for the care he gave him. Bowser had found a home.

CHAPTER SIX

The Bees' Nest

One thing Jack did not like was bees. He had been stung too many times to even want to be around them. He had killed many bees as a boy, especially bumble bees, because they would be flying around and lighting on the clover in the school yard. He and the other boys would have great fun stomping bees. It was funny to the other boys when one of them finally got stung and that usually ended the fun for the day. Of course, they'd go back to it another day, usually before school or at recess when they were just waiting to go inside and were kind of bored.

Jack had also been stung by honey bees. Lots of honey bees. He and his brother and sisters went barefoot most of the summer and were sure to step on an unsuspecting honey bee while it was collecting pollen. They always made the kids pay for their mistake. You only step on bees if you have shoes on! The victim's foot would have a red spot and some swelling would come up immediately. Sometimes the stinger would even get stuck in their foot. That always led to calls for help.

"Get that stinger out! Please! Ouch! Ouch! Ouch!" and so it would go. The truth is bee stings never left lasting damage and were usually forgotten in a day or two. It was all just part of growing up out in the country.

Sometimes a wasp would get in the house and sting one of them, sometimes it seemed just for meanness, especially those big red wasps. They were terrifying to look at and just the thought of getting stung by one of those monsters kept even the bravest kids on edge.

Then, of course, if you let your mind ramble, get to thinking about the meaner bees. Yellow jackets lived in the ground and if you happened to be playing or working around their nest, which was just a hole in the ground, usually hidden by grass grown up around it, you would not soon forget it! When they stung a kid, they really popped! Anytime a yellow jackets' nest was found, they'd run right quick and get some gasoline and pour down the hole. Gasoline will kill anything!

Some people might say, "Well, now, that's not good for the soil", and they'd be right, but when it came to yellow jackets, Jack and his family just wanted them gone. They'd think about the soil later.

So, it's like I said, Jack did not like bees. He had been stung too many times. There is one other kind of bee that usually made its nest in a tree or sometimes under the eaves of someone's house. These black bees were always angry, it seemed. They were called hornets.

One summer day, when the kids were out of school and there was work and play a plenty, Jack had a run in with some hornets that he would never forget. Now Jack had been stung by lots of different kind of bees, but somehow, up to this summer, he had never been hit by a hornet sting. That was all about to change.

Oh, he had seen them, and he had heard from his brother, Dan, and his little sister, Tommy, how bad their stings hurt, but he had never been stung by one. Of course, his little sister cried when she got stung, two times, one on the back of her neck and another time just under her right arm, but when Dan got stung…Well, he didn't exactly cry but he was yelling, "Ouch!" so loud it sounded like he'd been hit by a hammer and his eyes teared up some. Jack sure did not want to get stung by one so he kept his distance from the buzzing monsters. One time, Bowser got a hornet wrapped up in his fur, back on his hind quarters. He danced around and snapped at the bee. Finally, Dan was able to get a hold on her and slap the bee dead and then extract it from Bowser's coat.

Hornets! You've probably seen these cute pictures or cartoons that show hornets chasing people and it's all funny to watch. Maybe you've even seen a nest your teacher or uncle or somebody brought in to show off. After the bees have moved out of it, of course. But until you've been stung by a hornet, in my opinion, you've not really been stung. Let me tell you what happened.

You see, Jack was down in the pasture, where the spring stream flows and lots of willow trees grow. The willow trees like the wetter soil, and sometimes that pasture bottom would get swamped out—that is, it would just be standing in water. That made it a good habitat for frogs and turtles, even cotton-tailed rabbits. In the evening, those frogs, along with the crickets and locust that live in the trees and grasses out in the country, would put on a concert. People think the country is a quiet place! Hardly, and especially at night. Whip-or-wills and night hawks, along with the barn owls—mercy! It is something else! But this noise is different from city noise. It doesn't drive you crazy. In fact, between the lot of them, if your window is open to catch the night breeze, they will sing you to sleep every time. It's like Mother Earth looking after her children.

Anyway, Jack was down there in the bottom pasture, catching frogs and crawdads out of the stream. He and his brother, Dan, were having a contest to see who could catch the most of each. Some people ate crawdads, but they were so small that the McKinney's never took to it. The frogs on the other hand, they were known to cook up some frog legs now and again if there was enough to fool with. Sometimes they would even cook up a snapping turtle but those guys were kind of wily and were mostly left alone. No need to lose a finger or a toe! So, Dan set up by the road, just under the bridge to try his luck, but Jack meandered his way further and further down from the lane that led to his house. He knew in a little while his momma would be calling him and the rest of the kids in to dinner, but that thought slipped right out of his mind. He had an old pickle jar he was using to catch the crawdads and the one frog he'd been able to get a hold of. He heard a big "Ridip" just a bit further down and then he saw this frog.

"Wow," Jack thought. "That thing's as big as my hand!" He just raised up from the stream and took a step toward the frog when his shoulder bumped into something. He suddenly heard this buzzing that just continued to swell and he looked up right into the opening of a huge hornets' nest! He must have been so into catching crawdads and then trying to get to that big frog that he hadn't heard them till now. Oh, but now he heard them! And before he could think what to do, he had been popped twice on the head, once on his forehead and once right at the nape of his neck. Jack floundered backwards, stumbling into the stream, dropping his jar of crawdads and that one frog that he had caught. He turned over on his stomach to get up and run and got stung again in the middle of his back and on the back of his left thigh! He was too startled and frightened to do anything but get out of that stream and race across that pasture towards the house.

Dan looked up to see his brother, Jack, flying across the pasture. "You catch any yet, Jack?" he called. Jack didn't even respond but flew up to the house, scampering quickly over the pasture fence.

"What in the world is the matter?" He called out again.

"Hornets!" Jack called back. "Hornets got me!"

It was right then that his Momma came out to call the kids in for dinner. "Jack! For heaven's sake, boy! What is the matter with you?" Jack had run straight into her arms and was saying so many words so fast that none of them made any sense. "Mercy, son. Settle down now," his Momma said and then she noticed the big whelks coming up on Jack's face and neck. "Good gracious, son. You sure have got into something. The way those whelks are raising up, I'd say you found a hornets' nest!"

"Momma, they found me! I raised right up into a hornet's nest. Dan and me were down in the bottom catching crawdads and frogs. I saw this really big frog and was about to catch it when I bumped into the hornet's nest. They stung me over and over, Momma! They burn something awful! You got anything to help ease the pain?" Jack pleaded, almost yipping.

"Did the hornets get you good, Jack? You sure flew out of that pasture?" Dan asked, grinning but also seeing that this was not really a laughing matter, at least not now. Jack was biting his tongue in order not to cry, the pain just seemed to be increasing, especially where they stung him in his head.

"He'll be alright, but you know very well what those hornets will do to you. I want you kids to stay away from that part of the pasture until we kill those things, you hear me? His momma said back, all the while taking Jack's shirt off so they could see where all the bees had stung him.

Jack's Daddy was often over at his parent's place, helping on the farm, but on this day, he was whittling on an axe handle back by the smokehouse. "Go up there to the smokehouse and have your Dad apply some of his tobacco to those stings. That tobacco will pull the poison right out."

"Yes, ma'am, I will," Jack said, and with that he tore off up to the smokehouse, his Dad, and waiting relief.

When Lloyd saw his boy come running up, he knew something was wrong. "See here, Jack, what's the problem boy, somebody get snake bit?"

Jack composed himself a little. He sure didn't want to be crying or whimpering in front of his dad. "Daddy, the hornet's got me. A bunch of times. The stings burn something awful and Momma said your tobacco would pull the poison out."

"Boy, looks to me like they got you and good. Here. You take this chaw of tobacco and put it where it hurts the most. I'll work up another chew and put it on your back. Don't worry, son. This will take care of it, but you got stung quite a few times. Don't be surprised if you get a headache or stomach ache from all that poison. I hate hornets, but they are a fact of life out here in the country. I'll go down there, here in a little while, and throw gas on their nest. Maybe I get rid of them for you. A boy oughtn't to have to give up catching frogs and crawdads for fear of getting stung to pieces, do you reckon?"

No sir, I reckon not. Thanks, Dad. I already feel better. I knew those devils hurt, the way Dan did when they got him, but I had no idea. Mercy! I'll be paying more attention next time; you can count on that."

"I'd say you will, boy. I'd say you will," Jack's dad said in response.

It's like I said at the beginning, Jack did not like bees. He had been stung too many times to suit himself. I bet it was a month or more before Jack could walk right. Not from the bee stings, but from his fear of getting hit by another hornet. Everywhere he went he'd peer left and right, especially around trees. He'd have his head scrunched down, looking something like a barn owl, turning his head, this way and that.

CHAPTER SEVEN

Momma

Jack's momma had red hair. She had beautiful red hair with freckles like the stars of heaven. She had life in her. Mercy, did she have life. Her kids with all their youthful vigor had to stay after it to keep up with Momma. And did those kids ever love her and she them. Jack figured there was not another woman on earth like his momma and, of course, he was right.

Jack's Momma's name was Mayme Alverta, but her kids never called her that. No sir. She was always Momma to them. Now the kids and Momma was living during what was called "The Great Depression." Let me tell you, they had some hard times. For a time, Jack and his family lived in factory housing in Englewood. It was on what they called "Shootin' Street" and it didn't have that name for nothing. These houses were built to house the sock factory workers in town. People would come out of the mountains to find work to feed their families and sometimes they were a rough crew. Like I said, they didn't call it "Shootin' Street for nothing. Sometimes there would be fights out on the street, way up in the night, and Mayme would do her best to keep her children asleep, telling them it would be alright and God would take care of them, not to worry. Then she might be found praying on her knees till the danger passed and she could finally lay her weary head down for an hour or two of sleep before the sun rose and work began again.

It was a blessing from God that they had finally got out of the factory housing and were able to buy this little white house out in the country. Momma bought this house with some land from old Mrs. Pangle for a good price. You see, in those days land and homes sold for cheap because didn't nobody have any money. So, when Momma took in sewing and washing, she put her money away, as much as she could, and then there was the money her boys, Jack and Dan, brought in from cutting firewood and hiring out to help farmers nearby. The girls, Jean, and Margaret, and Denny, and Tommy, also helped bring in money by helping with the sewing and washing, and by helping with the crops they raised out on the place which they were able to sell from time to time to the folks in town. The fact is, when Momma set her mind to something, it got done. She used to say, "Kids, I want you to always remember, we are AmeriCANS not AmeriCAN'TS." She had lots of funny little sayings like that. But the kids got it, and Jack always knew, if it could be done, they would get it done and not rely on anyone else to carry their load. Momma instilled that in all her kids. A pridefulness that could only be matched by the brightness of her beautiful, fiery red hair.

Jack's momma knew how to read and write, which was something many people in her day were not able to do. Out in the knobs, in the hills, up in the mountains and other rural areas there weren't many schools and when there was school, they only met a few months out of the year. Kids were needed at home to help with chores, or crops, or getting in firewood, and other such things. She was pleased to say that she went through the third grade. It was actually called making it through the third reader back then. There was just so much to do back then and her stepdad, Gordon Dye, was a hard man. He worked hard and expected everyone else to do the same. To him, book learning was just foolishness and it didn't put bread on the table. You see, Mayme's dad, John Miller, died of appendicitis when she was only six years old. How her momma and sisters had loved that man. To her dying day she treasured the memory of him. But as time went on, her momma needed a man in her life and Gordon dye, whose wife had died and who needed help in raising his several children, came along and married her. It wasn't seen as fit in those days for a woman to be as young as Mayme's mother, whose name was Rilla Ann, to not have a husband to "look after her." Anyway, it was him who put a stop to Mayme's learning. She understood the negative aspect of being a stepchild from him.

As I was saying, everybody heated with coal or firewood back then. Most people even cooked on woodstoves and heated their bath water on the woodstove. If you are familiar with Amish communities today, then you might have a picture of how they lived in those days. It wasn't a bad way, but it was a hard way. It made for people of strong character and faith.

Every night Momma would read the Bible to her children and have them take turnabout reading it to the whole family. The kids learned to read as much at home as they did at school, and that from a woman who had a third-grade education. What might she have become if she had been able to continue her education? She was such a brilliant woman. Still, God has his ways and no matter the situation, "all things work together for the good to them that love God, to them who are called according to his purpose," the Good Book says. Mayme believed that with her whole heart. That's the bottom line. Momma always said, "We'll make do with what we have. If it's broke, we'll fix it. If we don't have it, we'll make it. Where there's a will, there's a way," and she meant it. It was this philosophy of life that guided all that they did. It was more than just Momma's way. It was the way of the old people. They had no hand outs and wanted none. God gave them the strength to get up in the morning and stay up at night, if need be, to do the things they needed to carry on. And so much more than that. It wasn't just what they did, it was the attitude and spirit in which they did it. They were always pushing for more and better so their kids would not have to struggle so, but there was purpose in the struggle. They lived their lives to honor God. The whole concept of God was far above them and they knew it, but they knew that there was One greater than them. It was the same One that gave them the fire in their belly to stay with the work long after their muscles burned with the effort. Jack's momma and their family were not the only ones who possessed this fire, but they modeled it beautifully. Every night when they went to bed there was a peace and contentment that settled inside them. It was an assurance that tough as this life was, they were headed in the right direction. They did not know where this course was taking them but they had faith in God that their final destination would not be a disappointment.

These little insights let you know something of who Jack's momma was. She was more than just the momma of six kids growing up in hard times. She was the firelight that they came home to, long after they grew up and had homes of their own. Her foundation of faith showed them how to live, no matter where they chose to live. Long after Jack's momma was gone on from this life, he and all his siblings held her up on the pedestal that is reserved for mothers.

Jack's momma had red hair. She had beautiful red hair with freckles like the stars of heaven. She had life in her. Mercy, did she have life.

There is a little poem by Margaret Widdemer that belongs right here. It expresses the heart of a mother, and seems to especially apply to Jack's momma, Mayme Alverta.

"The Watcher"

She always leaned to watch for us
Anxious if we were late,
In winter by the window
In summer by the gate.
And though we mocked her tenderly
Who had such foolish care,
The long way home would seem more safe,
Because she waited there.

Her thoughts were all so full of us,
She never could forget,
And so, I think that where she is
She must be watching yet.

Waiting 'til we come home to her
Anxious if we are late
Watching from heaven's window
Leaning from heaven's gate.

CHAPTER EIGHT

Aunt Thelma

Back in the days when Jack was growing up, people had big families. Some people had really big families of 12 or 13 kids, sometimes even more. There were 11 in Jack's daddy's family even. Because that was so, Jack had lots of aunts and uncles. His favorite of all his aunts and uncles alike was his Aunt Thelma. Aunt Thelma was his daddy's sister. She was number ten of eleven born to the family, so she was just a few years older than Jack. She was so full of life and fun that any time they saw Aunt Thelma coming down the road they'd leave whatever they were doing and run out to greet her.

Aunt Thelma loved to play games with the kids. She'd play hours in the woods with the girls, making believe that they had a house there and their own families. The other adults would visit on the porch, always talking about old times when they were kids, but Aunt Thelma was still living like she was a kid herself. Sometimes they'd get together a softball game and she would be right in the middle of them, pitcher for both teams. When Aunt Thelma was around, the kids' daddy was a little gentler and even their own sweet mother was inclined to smile more. Everybody loved Aunt Thelma but Jack liked to think that he was just a little more special than the other kids to her and, although he loved his other aunts and uncles, that she was just a little more special to him.

One day when Jack was out by the barn splitting wood for the winter, he looked up from his work to see Aunt Thelma skipping down the road toward him. She was singing a little song: "Bye Baby Bunting" it was called. It was a song that many mothers sang to their babies to help them calm down and go to sleep.

"Hey, Aunt Thelma, how are you on this fine day?" Jack asked. "What you singing that old lullaby for? You fixing to have yourself a baby?" He teased.

"No, Mr. Jack, I'm not about to have any babies to take care of. You'd be enough to take care of, if I had to take care of a baby. But I know somebody that is about to have a little baby and I'm not telling," she said with finality.

"Aww, now, that's not fair. You come skipping up the road singing a lullaby and then tell me somebody's going to have a baby and then you clam up on me. I'll just ask Momma who and she'll tell me," Jack said back defiantly.

"No, it won't do you any good, because she doesn't know herself. I just now found it out and came to tell your momma this very minute. So, see, Mr. Jack, you ain't so clever yourself," Aunt Thelma said back. She loved having this over him and, truth be told, Jack loved playing this little game of cat and mouse more than he cared who was going to have a baby. Lots of guys were like him. These kinds of details were just not that interesting to them. In fact, right at that moment, when Jack was splitting wood, he was imagining himself as Paul Bunyan, the biggest man in America. He was planning to load this wood onto Babe, the blue ox, just as soon as he finished getting it all cut. Such fantasies as these helped the work go by quicker and even made him look forward to it. Nevertheless, for the fun of it, he kept on at his Aunt Thelma.

"I'll tell you what," Jack offered. If you tell me who it is that is going to have a baby, I'll tell you who my brother Dan's girlfriend is."

Aunt Thelma seemed interested. "Dan's got a girlfriend? Mmmm, mercy. Does your momma and daddy know? We'll tease him unmercifully! First comes love, then comes marriage, then comes baby in a baby carriage!"

"Yeah, yeah, all that stuff. And you can spread it all over Englewood, but first you have to tell me who's going to have a baby," Jack responded.

Aunt Thelma seemed to be mulling it over. Suddenly her eyes got bright and she said, "Deal! Well, the baby is due to be born in February and its name is going to be…" Jack interrupted her. "I don't give a Rat's Vein for what its name is going to be or when it's going to be born or who it will grow up to marry. I just want to know who it is that is going to have a baby," Jack said impatiently.

"My, my," Aunt Thelma said back. "Look whose mister impatient. Okay, Okay. The baby will be born in February to a Mrs. Louise Seay!"

"Mrs. Seay! Our school teacher! She's going to have a baby! I love Mrs. Seay, but I don't guess I knew teachers could have babies. Teachers are teachers, they're not like the rest of us."

"Well, I never thought about it like that. But yes, Mrs. Seay, your teacher, can be a mother, too. She will be a fine momma," Aunt Thelma said. Then, she should her head with finality and went on. "Yes, I bet she'll make a good one. At least her baby will be the smartest kid around, don't you think?"

"Well, I guess so. Somebody has to be smart around here. I guess it's better to be smart than a smart aleck," Jack said, teasing.

"Yeah, yeah, whatever you say. Now what about Dan's girlfriend?" Aunt Thelma asked back. "Who is it? I bet it's that Martin girl."

"No, you got it wrong. Guess again," Jack teased.

"Well, he was hanging around with that Juanita Casteel the other day. Is it her?" Aunt Thelma guessed again.

"No, no, no. Not even close. You get one more guess," Jack said in response.

"Okay then. Only one more guess so I better get this one right. Old rascal that you are you might not even tell me after you promised and everything. Hmmm, I think I have been noticing that Land girl making big moon eyes at Dan. How's that for a guess?" Aunt Thelma said, smiling back at Jack with big moon eyes herself.

"Aunt Thelma! You knew all along. How did you figure it out?" Jack asked.

"A girl just knows things. We're not like you silly men, always thinking you know everything and paying attention to nothing!" Aunt Thelma said.

"Hummph!" Jack snorted back. "Whatever you say, Aunt Thelma, whatever you say," Jack responded, trying to sound upset with her but there was a slight grin on Jack's face. Though he was just barely a teenager by then, she had said "You silly men" and had included him in those who knew nothing. Strange as that might sound, it made him feel big and good about himself. Aunt Thelma had the power to do things like that. To make Jack or anyone else for that matter, feel a little bit more about themselves after spending time with her.

Just then, Bowser came out of nowhere and started barking at Aunt Thelma.

"Well now, who have we got here?" She asked kneeling down to pet Bowser. His tail was wagging to be the band. She had that way about her, even animals trusted her, somehow reading her nature and knowing a friend when they saw one.

"That's our new dog, Bowser. He's a fine dog, but he was an awful mess when he first came here. Somebody dropped him off, you know the way they do. He had the mange terrible bad. But we got the burnt oil out and rubbed him down good. We fattened him up a bit and he's turned out to be a pretty good dog," Jack said, rubbing his dog down good as Aunt Thelma petted his head and neck.

"He sure is a lively one. I like him. You're a good boy, aren't you?" She said to Bowser.

"Ruff, ruff!" Came his response. Bowser had found another friend.

CHAPTER NINE

Dad

Some people didn't even know that Jack had a dad. It was just always Momma and the kids, Dan and Jack, and Jean and Denny, and Margaret and Little Tommy. But there was a dad for their family and his name was Lloyd. Lloyd had been born a twin to Floyd but Floyd died in the Great War before the kids were old enough to know him. Like his brother, he was handsome and tall, with blue eyes and jet-black hair. There were eleven kids in Lloyd's family when he grew up in the Patty community. It was a small farming community outside of Riceville, a town on the other side of the county from where Jack and his brother and sisters grew up.

Jack's daddy was often in Patty working with his daddy, Jim. His name was James but everybody called him Jim. James' daddy, William, had been born in 1813 and was from North Carolina. He had moved out to McMinn county to find a place where his business could prosper. He was a blacksmith, and the little town in which he grew up and in which he had been an apprentice already had a blacksmith. William heard about cheap land and need for a blacksmith in a little town in east Tennessee which was called Riceville. So, he brought his wife and several kids with him and started a new life. That's how James and his family came to live in those parts. As for Lloyd's momma, her name was Alta Kay. Everybody called her Alta Kay, never just Alta. Alta never knew what her name meant, but no one else had the same name and she was glad. She always knew that if she heard the name Alta Kay it was her, they were referring to. Her momma had heard the name in a story that was told by the family hearth when she was a little girl. The man telling the story was her own Uncle Clem, and he was as Scottish a man as you would ever want to meet. His brogue was strong and one had to pay close attention to get every word. He told of a girl named Alta Kay, who came from the old country. She was so lovely that some said she may have once been a mermaid that had risen up out of the sea and made her home among the common folk in the glen. She had the gift of raising people up out of their despair. She was a bright light of hope in a country that was continually being kept down by the English. She lived in the high country of Scotland and could take people from the depths of despair to the silver lining of hope. She was just like that. She became a symbol of the high hope that she said was born within each of us. Her uncle had said that her name Alta meant "high" and that Kay meant "rejoice." Stories were often told by the fire back in those days. It passed the time, especially during the long winter months. Alta was a Caldwell when she married, but her momma's name is lost in time. Nevertheless, it was she that mulled over the name and decided at that point that if she ever had a little girl, she would name her Alta. She never got around to telling Alta where her name came from or what it meant because the old people often kept things to themselves. That was the way of the old people. They were like that when they came from the old country and that is the way they lived and died. Maybe it was because they had lived such hard lives in the place where they lived before. Maybe they thought it would bring bad luck if they hoped for too much for their children. And Alta's momma did have such big dreams for her children, and especially her first born, Alta. Her name meant "High" and came from the Spanish, its origins is found in the high grace of Mary, the mother of Jesus. Alta's mother knew that, but Alta Kay never did. Back in those days there were no computers or smart phones to look the meaning of things up quickly, and, of course, there were no public libraries. Even the private libraries were mostly burned up from when the Federal Army had march through so long ago, burning and destroying things in their wake. Thankfully, the old people spoke little of these things also. What was the point? The past was past. Now there were only the dreams of a brighter tomorrow and so mothers from the South named their kids hopeful names like "Alta" even if they were afraid to speak their hopes out loud.

So maybe knowing that will help you understand the importance of Jack's dad's name. Lloyd is an old Welch name that means "Grey", but it goes on back even to the Middle Ages where it means something like holy or set apart for God's service. When you have a name like that it sure is hard to live up to it. Lloyd thought so anyway. He might have felt the love behind the name his mother gave him. He might have felt the dream she had for her son. What mother does not want their child to be more? More than they were, more than what society said must come of children of poor farmers. So, Alta Kay dreamed as her mother had, and Jack's dad struggled with the high calling of his name.

Jack's own name was one that was full of hope from his own momma, Mayme. It meant "Grace" but was also connected to the Celtic meaning of "energy, full of energy." Did Jack ever live up to the 'full of energy' part! And like most of us, Jack could never fully grasp the full meaning of grace, but his life was awash with grace, every day of his life. His mother named him well.

Jack's dad, Lloyd, was often in Patty helping his daddy, Jim, farm the little piece of ground the family owned there. Farming was hard work but Jim was born for it. His boy, Lloyd wasn't as crazy about it as his dad was but he was crazy about his dad. And so, he worked with him, maybe even to the neglect of his own family, because daddy needed him. Sometimes the farmers would all gather up at Trew's General Store and tell the tales that farmers tale and complain of too much or not enough rain and of course, the price of crops going up and down, year to year, like a yoyo. Farming was tough. James' older brothers took to the blacksmith trade, after their daddy, but James had been influenced by the farmers in the area and had cast his lot to farming. So as was often the case, Lloyd was over in Patty helping his daddy with the farm. His daddy needed him.

Jack kind of knew how he felt. Jack sure needed his daddy. All kids do. They need a man who will be there to teach them how to do things. They need a model, an example they can follow. Most kids would take a bad example of a father rather than no example at all. So, when Jack's dad was around, his kids hung on him like ducks on a June bug. Kids just love the idea of loving their dad, so they are very forgiving. At every chance they got they enriched their daddy's world with their love. Lloyd, often beleaguered with the work of helping his dad, found their welcome home and embracing love a pleasant relief and a balm for his sore spirits.

The family lived out in the country, almost exactly between Englewood and Mecca Pike. If there is one thing a family in the country needs it's a cat. Cat's keep mice out of the house and in the country, there are lots of mice that love to chew on clothes and food that a poor family can't afford to give up to the little poachers.

So, one day when Jack's dad came home from his folk's farm in Patty, he had a little meowing kitten in his pocket. The children were all mesmerized by it immediately. It had such beautiful green eyes! Its fur was grey. It was no bigger than a shoe, but he was immediately adopted by the big open hearts of the children. The poor thing could hardly breathe as the kids struggled to get time to hold him and pet him and love him.

"What are we going to name him?" They all asked at once.

"Let's name him 'Tom'," Dan offered. "He is a boy cat after all."

"We can't name him Tom, Dan," Margaret protested. We already have a Tommy in our family. At that everyone turned to look at little Tommy. She was smiling, happy for the attention of all.

"What do you think we should name her, Little Tommy?" Jack said.

"Coco!" She burst out.

"Coco? Hmmm. I think I like it," Denny said.

"Me too! Me too!" came their united reply.

"Yeah for Coco!" said their dad. "Coco it is!" His baby daughter, Tommy, was named after his middle name, Thomas, and so she always had a special place in his heart.

When Tommy suggested "Coco" as a name for the cat, for some reason this made them all so happy they began to dance around and hug each other.

"Happy times come from simple things," Jack thought. "Why, this was nothing more than a stray kitten his dad had picked up and brought home thinking it might make his kids happy and they could use it as a mouser—that one act of thoughtfulness transformed the day from typical to something special," he mused.

"This is great!" Jack's brother, Dan, said. And those three words described perfectly how they all felt. Coco, the kitten, soon to be Coco, the cat, the mouser around the place, proved to be just one more piece of the puzzle that is family and Coco fit the part perfectly. Jack's dad, Lloyd, smiled. He felt that he was anything but 'holy" as his name implied. He knew that a good dad would be around more and he was torn by the duties and opportunities that he found between his parents and his wife and children. Maybe one day he'd figure out a proper balance, but for this moment he felt peace. He felt love. He felt like he had stepped up to bat and hit this one out of the park! So, for this moment, at least, he decided to bask in the glow of being dad.

CHAPTER TEN

The Dream

It was sometime after this that Jack had a dream that was one of those transitional dreams where everything just kept transforming into something else. Now, Jack was bad to dream. Every night he would have dream after dream, often waking him up and then leaving him trying to remember the details of the dreams. He dreamed of people he had never met before and then later, sometimes, he'd hear those very names called when he would be walking down the road in town. The very faces of the people he had dreamed about.

"Weird," Jack would think. One time he dreamed that he was the president of the United States and lived in Louisville, Kentucky, not Washington, D. C. Jack had these weird dreams and had no answer for them. Sometimes folks would say, "It's because you ate too late," or "It comes from working too hard," or "You're just full of the devil, that's what." Jack decided it would just be better to keep his dreams to himself. In the mornings when he got up, if his family asked him if he'd had any more of those weird dreams, he'd just say, "Nah. I reckon I must have been sick or something. I don't have any dreams at all anymore." This was the farthest thing from the truth, but at least folks didn't make fun of him or think he was going crazy or something.

Jack thought that his having to keep his dreams to himself might be like people who wanted to do something with their lives but were afraid to express it for fear of being harassed about it. He'd find out later that verbally expressing one's goals was the first step to making them reality. Maybe that was why so many lived desperate and depressed lives. Their hopes and aspirations were all locked up inside until they withered and died. Later in life Jack would find this nugget of truth and use it to propel him far beyond what anyone would have imagined for him. Dreams might be weird. They might not click or register with other people. But dreams and goals are specially crafted within the heart of the one who has them. Expression of those dreams is necessary to discover one's true self.

When Jack was an old man, he finally realized these things, but at this point in his life, he was just a poor country boy who woke many a night from weird dreams.

Now Jack and his brother, Dan, always slept in the same bed. With eight people in a two-bedroom house they had to work something out. The boys' bedroom was just off the living room. Their mom and dad's bedroom was just off the kitchen, and they had built in the back porch to make two additional small bedrooms for the girls to sleep in. Those bedrooms were so small the mice felt cramped in them. Still, it worked and no one complained really. Everybody they knew had at least one other person sleeping in the bed with them. It wasn't weird, it was just the way it was.

The Millers were their cousins and they lived a couple of knobs away from Jack's family. The Millers were a few years older and some of them had already taken off to serve in the army. So, one day Momma's sister, Ellie, came by in their buckboard with a big bunkbed loaded in the back. Her son, Earl, was riding with her.

"Well, Ellie, Earl," Momma called up to them. "What are you two out doing this morning? What's that you've got in the buckboard there?"

Earl jumped down and gave his Aunt Mayme a hug. "Aunt Mayme, we've got a bunk bed here that me and Kenneth used to sleep on, but we've outgrown it and we brought it over here hoping maybe your boys could use it."

"Well, let's see here, nephew. That sure is a fine-looking bunk bed, Ellie, and I am sure the boys would love it, but we can't afford to be buying something so nice when the boys have got a bed already to sleep in."

Ellie responded, "Now, Mayme, we aren't wanting to sell this bed. We just needed to get it out of the house to give us more space. You'd be doing us a favor to take it. No cost except to help us get it unloaded out of this buckboard." Ellie knew Mayme was poor but proud and would not want to accept charity, but if she thought she was helping Ellie out, that would be different.

"Why, sure, Ellie. We'll help you get that thing unloaded. The boys will love it and that way we can give their bed to the girls. It has a real mattress on it and not those pokey straw ticks.

Jean had come up out of the yard just then, in time to hear that they'd be getting a real mattress in place of their straw tick. "Oh, my! Really? Oh, Aunt Ellie, I could just kiss you!" And at that she ran around and jumped right up on the wagon and kissed her Aunt, good and sugary, on her left cheek.

Aunt Ellie was taken aback. "Well," she stammered. "Mayme, I knew the boys would be excited, but I didn't figure on the girls being so excited!"

"It is a fine day for sure, Ellie. We all appreciate it," Mayme responded.

That night, Dan and Jack actually went to bed early. Every night they wanted to stay up later. They weren't the kind to back talk their folks, but what boy wants to go to bed when he's young? Who knows what might be missed?

Mayme smiled when the boys hurried off to bed that night. The new bed was like a toy to them, and they were excited to try it out.

Dan and Jack stayed awake for who knows how long, whispering about how much better this bed was and weren't they lucky? Jean and Denny got their old mattress and were as excited as the boys, but Margaret and Tommy still had to sleep on straw ticks. Both the boys decided that when they got enough money saved up, they would buy their little sisters a real mattress too. This thought helped ease their conscious, and allowed them to slip off to sleep.

Sometime in the night Jack, who had the top bunk, began to dream. His dreams flowed like a river from one thought to another but they were somehow connected. He dreamed of swimming in the Tellico River, and seeing this kid jump off a rock way out in the river. The kid couldn't have been more than seven or eight years old and pretty soon it was clear that the kid didn't know how to swim. Jack jumped in the river, swam over and took hold of the kid and pulled him to safety. Then Jack realized he wasn't at the Tellico River but climbing Buzzard Roost, a high knob a couple of miles from their house. He was with several other people he did not know. Why he was with them he couldn't tell. Suddenly he heard a girl screaming! She had slipped and barely was able to hold on to a root anchored on a rock at the top of a bluff. The girl could hold on, but Jack knew she did not have the strength to pull herself up. He reached over the bluff as far as he could and pulled her up, as he did, he found that he had lost his balance and hold and was now dangling on the edge of the bluff! But Jack realized that he was not hanging on the bluff now, but he was swinging on a vine in the woods behind their house. Dan was swinging on a vine a few trees over and they were having a great time. Suddenly, there was a crack and Jack saw that Dan was in trouble. His vine was slipping and now they weren't in the woods any longer but hanging over an empty space that seemed to have no bottom. Jack quickly took off his shirt and tied it to the tree where the vine held and then reinforced his efforts by taking off his pants and tying them on in another place to ensure that the vine did not give way letting Dan fall. Jack reached down and took hold of Dan's vine. Somehow Jack was above Dan now so he tried to swing the vine so that Dan came over to the edge and was able to catch hold and pull himself to safety. Jack pulled and pulled. The vine began to swing more and more and finally Dan was able to catch hold. As he did, Jack, who had overextended himself to get the vine to swing in enough for Dan to dismount, lost his grip and tumbled down to the forest floor. As he did, he saw that he was going to land on a white rock! He squeezed his eyes shut and made impact! Jack came up off the floor, holding his back and yelling, "Oh, oh, oh!"

Dan was startled awake. "What in the world are you doing?" He asked. "You fell off the bed, didn't you?"

Jack, embarrassed and frustrated, said, "Well, I was trying to save you from falling and this girl from falling and this boy from drowning and...Oh..." He looked at Dan's grinning face. "Oh, just forget about it and go back to sleep."

Dan gave him this devilish grin. "You're having those crazy dreams again."

"Dan, don't tell momma and the girls. They'll give me a hard time over it," Jack pleaded.

"Don't worry, old brother. Some things just need to be kept between us. Besides, I reckon you can't help it. You're just a little bit crazy is all. Everybody knows that already," Dan teased.

"Well, I reckon your right about that. I appreciate you not telling," Jack said, rubbing his back.

After a moment, Jack called up meekly to his brother, "Hey, Dan. You want to switch beds?"

CHAPTER ELEVEN

The Sea Turtle

Jack was out with his friend, Winston, a week or so after the dream and his falling out of bed. He told Winston about he and Dan getting a new bed, but he left out the part about his crazy dream and the rest. Your friends don't have to know everything. Anyway, they were walking along the Conasauga Creek, which ran near Mecca Pike, the road from Etowah to Tellico. Winston was a Harris who lived in Englewood. The boys had gone to school together. Winston had a brother named Tap who was usually with him, just like Dan was usually with Jack but for whatever reason their brothers were not with them on this day.

Jack and Winston had been down at the creek fishing and had a string of trout to take home. They were just about ready to head home when Jack said, "Hey, Winston, let's jump in a while and cool off." Winston sure didn't need to be pushed in. He had his clothes peeled off and was in the water before Jack had even put down the string of fish. "Mercy, I reckon you must have wanted to cool off worse than me!" Jack exclaimed, but his words were lost in his own splash in the water as her jumped in, the water just about waist deep.

"You know what, Jack?" Winston asked.

"What?" Jack said in reply.

"This here water is just about right for baptizing in, I reckon, and you look to me like a good candidate!" And at that Winston threw Jack back in the water, both of the boys laughing their heads off.

"Gee, thanks," Jack said. "Having my sins washed away is a good thing but a little longer and you'd have sent me straight to heaven!"

"Hey, Jack, if you make it there before me, will you be sure and come back and tell me what it's like?" Winston teased.

"Well, I reckon I could do that, Winston," Jack said. "But it won't do you any good to know, because you aren't going there unless…" and at that Jack grabbed his friend and plunged him under the water! Winston clambered out of the water, sputtering. Both boys were laughing now, having had their practice at baptizing and being baptized. They put their arms around one another's shoulders and were about to climb up the creek bank when Jack spotted something out of the corner of his eye.

"Look there, Winston! What is that?" Jack asked.

Winston said, "Well, I'll be, Jack! That looks like a turtle, but if it is, it is the biggest one I've ever seen." Winston started toward it and Jack held him back.

"Easy now, Winston. Let's figure this out. We don't want him getting away. Let me get out and go down the creek a little way and when I say go, we'll both start walking toward him. That way one of us is bound to catch him."

"You don't reckon it's a big snapping turtle, do you, Jack?" Winston asked.

"I sure never seen one so big if it is," Jack responded.

"You don't guess it's one of them sea turtles Old Mrs. Seay was telling us about in school a little while back, now do you?" Winston asked. Now neither of these boys, Jack or Winston, paid a whole lot of attention at school, but when Mrs. Seay showed the class that picture of the sea turtle, she had all the kids' attention.

Johnny Bain said, "Mercy, Mrs. Seay, Is them real?"

"Are they real?" Mrs. Seay corrected.

"That's what I'm asking you," Johnny retorted.

A bit exasperated, but always pleasant, Mrs. Seay said, "Why, yes, Johnny, they are real. They are related to the family of turtles we see around here, box turtles and snapping turtles, but they are much bigger. Some of them will go as big as a truck tire and they can swim in the water like nobody's business."

"Well, I'll be." Jack said after thinking about the picture in Mrs. Seay's book and the discussion they had in class. "Winston, that has to be one of them sea turtles, but how in the world did it get here in this creek? The ocean is forever away."

Winston thought a minute. "Somebody had to put it here, and that's fine with me because I aim to get me a ride on that sea turtle!" Just then, as if the turtle understood what the boys were talking about, it made a dart to get past Jack. In that moment, he caught the turtle, sort of accidentally by the fin. The momentum of the turtle pulled him so hard that he flipped around and was somehow riding on the back of that turtle, both hands anchored on the shoulder of a fin!

Winston yelled, "Woohoo! Jack! Ride him, Jack!" and "Hey, hold up! I want a turn!" Jack's eyes were as big as saucers! He was having the time of his life and the bliss of it caught him by such a surprise that he found himself quite speechless. Winston thought maybe something was wrong and so he called out, "Jack, you okay? That thing doesn't have you by the leg, does he?" Just then the turtle turned back sharply and threw Jack off, swimming past Winston and down the creek and was gone. The boys just looked at each other and then they started laughing and running after that turtle all at once! They looked and they looked, talking excitedly all the while. After an hour or so, they gave up and took their string of fish and walked home, worn out from their grand adventure but still giddy from all the fun they had had.

About the time they got back to the knobs where they lived, they got to wondering if anyone would even believe them. First that they had seen a sea turtle in a fresh water creek, and then second, that Jack had ridden the thing like a cowboy from the old West. There were no pictures, no video recordings. There was nothing to prove what they had seen and done, but they told it anyway. Everybody thought their story was a case of over imagination.

"Sure, you did. Umhmm. Whatever you say. You boys would tell anything to get out of trouble for coming home late." These were the kind of comments they got from their brothers and sisters, aunts and uncles. Jack's momma didn't know what to think of the boys' tale. It was quite a stretch, but she pondered it in her heart. You know, mommas know things that others don't. Somehow, they have this extra sense about them. Something told her, as strange as the tale was, it might just be true. Nobody else even gave their story time of day.

That night when the boys lay down in their beds, in their homes, Winston in the Town of Englewood, and Jack out in the knobs of Liberty Hill, they dreamed of a day like no other and thanked God, as they knew Him, for giving poor country boys, such as themselves, a day they'd never forget.

CHAPTER TWELVE

The Road

Jack loved being out at night. Sometime after his family had all gone to bed in the little white house where they lived, Jack would slide out quietly from his bed (he slept with his brother, Dan), slide into his overalls, and creep across the bedroom, through the living room, and off the porch to the fresh air outdoors that awaited him. The sparkling stars in the night sky awed him with the amazement of wonder that can only be seen through the eyes of a young boy and in the dark that can only be found away from the city lights.

Sometimes Jack would just ease out in the yard and lay down in the cool grass. From there he could take in a sky full of stars, seeming to swirl about him. Jack struggled to take in the beauty of it all. "How in the world could anybody ever be bored at night when God puts this kind of show on for everybody to see?" He thought to himself. Jack memorized the location of many of the stars and knew their alignment, so any time he found one constellation, he knew where to look for the others. Orion, the Pleiades, the Bear, and his favorite, the Archer. Many of the star constellations Jack felt were a stretch and wondered what the ones who named them where thinking when they saw this random grouping of stars and decided it was a bear or a fish or whatever. But the Archer was different. At least to Jack. He could just see that man with his bow taking aim at …what? Scorpio, somebody said, but try as he might, Jack never could make out a scorpion for the Archer to shoot.

Anyway, Jack and his brother, Dan, had made several bows, most of them not very good, but they liked to get some sticks and skin them off and sharpen the points, then get some kind of string, usually bailing wire, and see what they could hit with them. Within fifteen or twenty feet they could do alright, but after that the arrows would go all over the place and that made shooting them all the more fun. One time, Jack shot his arrow right into his sister Jean's blouse which their momma had hung on the clothes line to dry. Jack looked at Dan, Dan looked at Jack, and the boys quickly retrieved the arrow and ran behind the barn to hide. Both of them were breathing hard and doing their best to stifle their laughter so they weren't discovered.

Later, when Momma noticed the hole in Jean's blouse, she asked Jean about it. Of course, Jean had no idea how it had gotten in there. Momma looked closely at Jean for a moment and then sighed. "I guess it's a wonder all you kids' clothes aren't filled with holes. Most of these clothes have been handed down so many times that they're worn to a frazzle. Just lay it in my bedroom by the sewing machine. We'll see if we can't get a few squares out of it for the quilt we are working on." The boys sure dodged a bullet on that one. Not that Momma was mean or anything, but they, or at least Jack, would have probably gotten a whipping for ruining Jean's blouse. Momma always sent them down to the bottom pasture, where the spring stream ran and willows grew, to get themselves a willow stick to be whipped with if they misbehaved. Now these little willow branches could raise a welt on the back of your leg or across your back, and they stung some, but in a day or so the pain was forgotten and the welt was gone. Momma's discipline was not intended to cause the kids damage, but to give them a timely reminder to think before they acted. The Bible said, "Foolishness is bound in the heart of a child, but the rod of correction shall drive it far from him." Momma believed it. Sometimes her discipline worked better than others.

Jack woke up. He had been 'chasing rabbits' as the old folks called it. He let one thought lead to another then to another then to another and had dosed off to sleep under the faint light of the distant archer. He got up and stretched. He could see that the stars had shifted and he was a little stiff from the cool night air, but he still didn't want to go back inside and go to bed. He headed over to the main road that ran along the front of their property. Sometimes at night when he was cold, he would walk down the hill and back up the next hill to that road. The road would be warm from cars and wagons passing on it through the course of the day. It was packed dirt but somehow it held the heat of the day longer and when Jack laid down on it, he felt the heat radiate through his body and sooth him into a peace that was worth the walk to get there.

When Jack got over to the road, he could hear the crickets singing in the willow trees and the tree frogs making music along the stream. Between the two sounds and the lonesome call of the whippoorwills, the concert was marvelous and no ticket was required. The show was free, courtesy of the Creator of all things. As Jack laid himself down on the road, he felt the warmth ease up into him. He found again the Archer and studied his form. He took in the night sounds and felt himself blessed, blessed, blessed. "How good can life get?" He wondered just as he slipped off to sleep again.

He was dreaming of his dog, Bowser, who was normally so much fun to play with, but now, in his dream, he was tugging at him. Jack was tired and just wanted to rest, but Bowser barked and ran circles around him, reaching in to tug at his overall pants legs. "Leave me alone, Bowser. What's the matter with you, boy? I just want to rest. We'll play later." But Bowser would not leave or let him rest. He kept barking and tugging on him. "Okay, okay!" Jack said, and he woke up suddenly. He saw a light coming at him at high speed and impulsively rolled away from it into the ditch. He heard the engine roar as it passed and then sat up in time to see the tail lights fade and disappear as the automobile rounded the curve down below Jim Daugherty's place.

Jack realized that he had fallen asleep and just narrowly missed being flattened by that passing car. They would have never seen him. After all, most people are not looking for kids to be sleeping out on deserted roads late at night. "My goodness!" Jack thought. "Thank God for Bowser. He saved my life!" But where was Bowser? There was no sign of him anywhere. "Hmmm, that's weird," he thought. "I'd better get on back to the house and get laid down in a real bed before anything else happens," he said out loud to the night sky.

When Jack got back to the house, he found Bowser asleep on the front porch. He stirred as Jack settled himself beside him. "Hey, how did you get back here so quick? Thanks for waking me up over on the road. I'd have been smashed for sure." Bowser looked at him quizzically and then lay his head back down and went immediately back to sleep. Jack could see that the dog was not winded or panting. "How is it that he ran circles around me, tugging repeatedly on my pants leg and then came back home and fell sound asleep, not winded at all, in the time it took me to walk back to the house?"

Jack slipped back into the house and eased into the bed with his brother, Dan.

Dan stirred and asked sleepily, "Where you been?"

"I was over laying on the road, just feeling its warmth and like to got run over!" He waited for a response from Dan but he was already back to sleep. The bed felt good and cozy as he made his nest for sleep. "Wow! That was close," he thought to himself. "Weird about Bowser. Did that even really happen? Did Bowser wake me or did I dream that? Did God send Bowser to rescue me from my sleep? Sort of a spirit Bowser? Did it even happen at all? He looked at the knuckles on his left hand and saw that they were crusted from road dirt and knew he at least had been on the road. "Hmmm. It's like this is a God thing. People might not believe me, but I think God just saved my life." And Jack fell to sleep that night, much of what happened still a mystery, like the constellations in the sky.

CHAPTER THIRTEEN

Jack's Truck

I t was in the cool of the morning. Squirrels were chattering back and forth along the path the children walked. They mimicked the squirrel talk with their best clacking of tongue against the roof of their mouths. Little Tommy looked in wonder at her brothers who seemed to sound just like the squirrels in the trees. "How do you do that, Dan? How come you and Jack can sound so much like the squirrels? Show me how to do that?"

"You'll figure it out. One of these days your tongue will find the right place in your mouth and you'll be talking to squirrels anytime you want to. Just wait and see," Dan replied.

Jack just smiled at his little sister. The other girls had gotten wise enough to keep an eye on their older brothers. They were full of mischief and always pulling tricks or telling things that were just a little wide of actual truth. They did it all in fun, but the fun came at the expense of the one who was being played. The boys didn't do that little Tommy. At least not yet. She was so sweet and innocent they couldn't bring themselves to hurt her feelings by violating her trust.

Jack and Dan, were walking to school with their four sisters, Wanda Jean, Virginia Rhea, Margaret Ann, and Tommy Faye. Unlike the others, Jack didn't really like school. His brother and sisters weren't really crazy about it either, but they brought home better marks than he did. If it hadn't been for the learning part, Jack would have liked school just fine. It was always fun to play with their friends at recess and before and after school, but the learning part…It was kind of tough. Especially for Jack. He didn't like to read. He hated when it came his turn to read. He'd look down at the page and try to work the letters out. The teacher would say "Jack, it's your turn to read." "I know," he'd say. He would move his mouth and try to make the right sounds. Almost always he got it wrong and the other kids would snicker or smile quietly to themselves.

Sometimes a girl sitting nearby might offer help, whispering the words, but this only confused Jack more. The teacher would say "Jack, have you been practicing? You are never going to be a good reader unless you practice. How are you going to make it in the world if you can't read?" So, he'd try again and fail again. Over and over. So, you see why Jack didn't really like school. He said the words just jumped on the page every time he took a good look at them.

Now I've got to say that this wasn't Mrs. Seay. She had been Jack's teacher the year before. No, this year he had a man teacher, Mr. Kinard. He had moved to Englewood from somewhere up north. Maybe Virginia.

Anyway, one day when Jack had been called on to read yet again and yet again had failed, the kids were laughing and someone said "He'll never learn" and another boy said, under his breath because he really didn't want to get in a fight after school and he knew Jack was a fighter, "Jack too stupid to read". But Jack heard it. He heard it all and he yelled at the boy,

"You just wait till after school, Johnny Lintner. I'll be waiting for you out by the cedar grove. We'll see then what becomes of that mouth of yours." When the teacher heard Jack's plan and threat to Johnny, (though, Lord knows he was continually picking on people and all the kids knew he needed to be put in his place) well, the teacher just lost control of himself and started flogging him with the marking slate he picked up off Jack's desk. Jack came up out of his chair (he was only twelve or thirteen years old and maybe ninety pounds soaking wet) and pushed the teacher back and quick as a flash he jumped out the school house window and was gone.

He never went back to school. He'd had enough of being laughed at and feeling like he couldn't do anything right. They didn't know anything about dyslexia in those days. They just figured you must be slow or dumb if you couldn't learn to read. That Lintner boy did not get his whipping that day, but it did come, on another day, when Jack saw him picking on little Tommy, making fun of her red hair. Jack licked the tar out of Johnny and dared him to ever mess with one of his sisters again. If he did, no one ever told Jack about it.

Jack could have gone back to school and apologized to the teacher, (though it should have probably been the other way around) but he never did. He was done with school. Still, there was work to do. Jack began to help around a lumber yard loading rough cut lumber onto flatbed trucks. The lumberyard wasn't too far from the McKinney place so Jack could just walk into work. From time to time, he would ride Jenny, the family horse, but most often it was needed at the house, where it was used for plowing or pulling a supply wagon. Jack was just a boy but after jumping out the window of the school it was like he jumped into the world of being a young man. His folks hadn't had any education to speak of so they didn't press him on it. Besides, they needed the extra money Jack's work brought in. He was allowed to keep a portion of his earning and he kept the money stashed away in the barn in an old cigar box. He hid it under the hay and only went out to add to it. He never took any money out to buy himself or a maybe a girl he liked some candy. He was saving. Jack had a dream of a flatbed truck of his own. He figured if he had his own truck, he could cut trees and bring them into the lumber yard and sell them as an independent contractor. He'd make more money than he could as a lumber yard employee.

Jack couldn't read but he could add numbers up in his head as fast as anyone around. He had a plan and he worked his plan. The truck he had is eye on was a Chevrolet 3100 Flatbed. They cost just over eleven hundred dollars new, but he knew he could save the money if he kept at his work and saved ever cent he could spare. Jack was making around twenty dollars a week working at the lumberyard. He was proud to be able to help the family by giving half (and sometimes more) of his earning to his mother. He had some minor expenses, but by and large he was able to save ten dollars a week. In two and a half years, by the time he was fifteen, Jack took his cigar box to the Chevrolet dealership in Athens (the county seat) and bought himself a brand-new flatbed pickup truck. The money he had left over after his purchase was enough to buy a couple of chainsaws and other necessities for his business. As he figured, working for himself brought in much more money and, along with it, much more responsibility. He was on the road to being a man.

The day Jack drove that truck by the school was the proudest day of his young life. He honked the horn over and over. The young kids came out and jumped up on the running board and banged the inside of his truck doors! It was like they were all celebrating with him! He was a success despite everything, and everybody in that small town knew it. "How in the world?" they said out loud. That Jack must not be so dumb after all. "Reckon why it is he can't read?" Most of them would never know but they did take note that if a young man will set his mind to something, he can do it. No matter what folks say.

This is not the end of Jack's story. He had more adventures in his lifetime than could every be confined in the cover of a book. Still, this gives you an idea of who Jack was, what his family was like, and what the place and times were liked when he was young. Be sure to keep your eye out for further adventures in Jack's life. Little by little, maybe, we can get the main parts of his story told.

AFTERWARD

Jack's Story is, at least in part, based on actual events. However, the events are scrambled, using stories from several members of our family. They are multigenerational. Stories my Granny told are attributed to my Dad, and stories from other family members go to him as well. Some of these stories even come from my own life, now incorporated as 'Jack's Story.' A couple of these stories are completely from my imagination, but are told in historical context.

Most of the people in these stories are real, but some of them are out of their true time frame and, the truth be told, most of what is told here has been manufactured in the far-reaching places of my mind. I love my family and the East Tennessee area in which we were all born and raised. Because my purpose has been to shine a positive light on our people (We all have skeletons in our closets but we don't have to live in there with them!) I have focused on the funny and sweet moments I keep in my treasure chest of memories.

Thanks for reading.
Danny McKinney

ABOUT THE AUTHOR

Danny McKinney was born and raised in East Tennessee, in the foothills of the Appalachia Mountains. He has served as a minister, a middle school teacher, a courier for Fed Ex, a handyman, and is a bit of a shade tree mechanic. In addition to writing, he loves meeting new people and hearing their own stories of when they were young. He has been married to the former Rae Jean Stockberger for the past 40 years. They are the proud parents of three beautiful children (no matter what your age, you will always be your parents' children): Seth, Amanda, and Jessica. They are also the proud grandparents of Amanda's children: Owen, McKenna, and Karsyn. After many years of living and working in Southern New Mexico, the family is at home again in East Tennessee.

www.ingramcontent.com/pod-product-compliance
Lightning Source LLC
Chambersburg PA
CBHW051550120626
46551CB00013B/1459